To the saints of Heritage Baptist Church
in Manhattan, who demonstrate a passion
for God and faithful service to Him.
It is a privilege living on the edge of
eternity with you and laboring for
our Lord Jesus Christ in our nation's
largest and most strategic city.

Contents

Acknowledgments

My thanks go to Suzette Jordan of BJU Press for her encouragement in writing this book when I was ready to give up. I also thank her for her being a great copy editor with which to work. I greatly appreciate Antoinette Nwandu, a faithful member of Heritage Baptist Church, who read my initial drafts and provided invaluable help, corrections, and suggestions. Finally, I thank my wife, Debbie, who challenged me to write in such a way that hearts would be challenged to truly love and know God. I pray that her loving support to me will prove fruitful to assist everyone reading this book to live well on eternity's edge.

Introduction

Because I am convinced there is only one way to heaven through Jesus Christ our Lord, many times I hear an unbeliever pity my faith in Christ. They say things like, "It doesn't matter what you believe as long as you are a good and sincere person." Or "There are many ways to get to God, just like there are many ways to get to New York, by car, train, or airplane. We will all end up in heaven because all religions essentially say the same thing." Or "What about the billion Muslims in the world? You mean to tell me that they are all going to hell? What gives you the right to claim your religion is superior to theirs?" These statements demonstrate the belief that contradictory religious systems can coexist and be considered equally true.[1]

This common belief—that all religious systems are equally valid—is religious pluralism, and it may be the number one tenet held by "spiritual" but unsaved people today. One may think that the rise of religious pluralism is a uniquely modern phenomenon, but as we examine 2 Kings 2, we see that Elijah lived in a religiously pluralistic nation, the Northern Kingdom of Israel. The popular religions throughout his ministry were a counterfeit brand of Judaism and the heathen worship of a deity called Baal. That these counterfeit religions maintained equal status with God's law was an absolute evil in His sight (1 Kings 16:30–33). Realizing this will be vital to understanding the spiritual applications for the prophet Elijah's final day on earth. Elijah stood to proclaim the God of Abraham as the only true God and the law given by Moses as the authoritative Word from God. The very essence of evil in the land during his time was simply false worship. The living God, Who has not changed from the time of the Hebrew kings to this very day, is jealous and will not tolerate those who rival the worship of Him.

Great tension pervaded Israel about 853 BC as we arrive at Elijah's last day in 2 Kings 2:1–15. The once great nation of Israel had been divided in 931 BC—Israel in the north and Judah in the south. The nations surrounding Israel were polytheistic, recognizing many gods of varied functions who oversaw different aspects of life from birth to death, and the Northern Kingdom had been quickly overrun with some of these idolatrous ideas. Jeroboam, the first king of divided Israel, devised his own false religion and instituted a counterfeit of Judaism. He feared that his citizens would turn their allegiance to Jerusalem if they continued worshiping there, so he ordained two cities, Dan and Bethel, within his own country as proxy worship centers. This man-made religion centered on the carnal reasoning of Jeroboam's "own heart," which appealed to the people's desire for convenience (1 Kings 12:25–33). He ordained feast days and priests that were similar to those in the law of Moses but were not ordained by God. This was a great evil in God's sight, and the Lord predicted that He would destroy Jeroboam's house "from off the face of the earth" (1 Kings 13:34). False religion, mass murder, suicide, and drunkenness characterized the royal line after Jeroboam, which led finally to Ahab, the worst of the worst (1 Kings 15:26–16:28).

In 874 BC King Ahab ascended to the throne and married Jezebel, the daughter of a heathen king (1 Kings 16:29–34). Elijah the prophet appeared on the scene shortly after and served throughout and beyond Ahab's twenty-two-year reign. Ahab and Jezebel were ruled by absolute ambition; their marriage was a political alliance, not a caring relationship. Jezebel was from Phoenicia, Israel's flourishing seacoast neighbor, and this diplomatic union resulted in immediate—howbeit temporary—economic growth for Israel. Ahab was a builder, a statesman, and a warrior. He built Samaria and made it into a strong capital city (1 Kings 16:23–24). He constructed other cities and an ivory palace for himself and rebuilt the walls of Jericho (1 Kings 22:39; 16:34). He twice defeated powerful Syria in battle (1 Kings 20:1–34). In spite of these accomplishments, his union with Jezebel led Israel to ultimate ruin, for she reintroduced Baal worship into their nation (1 Kings 16:29–34).[2] Although Ahab and Jezebel both were extremely aggressive, Jezebel's cruel craftiness far exceeded the often weak Ahab. She had God's true prophets killed or driven into hiding, she plotted against godly citizens and had them murdered, she provided for the prophets of Baal, and she threatened Elijah with death (1 Kings 18:4; 21:1–16; 18:19; 19:4). Unquestionably, Jezebel exercised tremendous influence throughout Ahab's administration.

Baal was the supreme god of the nations surrounding Israel—the Babylonians, the Canaanites, and the Phoenicians—and serving him was hassle-free religion. Israel was no stranger to Baal.[3] This deity is also referenced in secular literature of that day. For Baal worshipers, life was cheap, and the economy was supreme. Baal promised the hope of prosperity and the pursuit of pleasure, but with a cost. Children were sacrificed for material success. The environment was valued above the souls of men. Moral absolutes did not exist. A main focus was on fertility. Licentious dancing along with sexual immorality of both male and female prostitutes took place and was widely practiced on "every high mountain and under every green tree" (Jeremiah 3:6). Worshipers valued the fruitfulness of their land, their livestock, and their women above loyalty to the Lord, Who created them.[4] Because of its inherent immorality, Baal worship was a religion of tolerance; the only people who could not be tolerated were men such as Elijah who held to absolute truth.

The combined influx of Baal worship and Jeroboam's imitation of Judaism transformed Israel into a pluralistic and profligate land. Elijah's narrow way to God through the law of Moses allowed no compromise with false faiths, and his battle against Baal was a part of a long confrontation throughout Hebrew literature between these two worldviews.[5] Elijah maintained loyalty to God and faithfully upheld the monotheistic worship of the one God Who created and controls the world.

Although Ahab and his successor and son, Ahaziah (2 Kings 1), were dead when Elijah awoke for his final hours, Baal worship and Jeroboam's false religion were not. In fact, the spiritual condition in the land had not improved after Elijah's lifetime of work; it was worsening as the ugly tentacles of idolatry continued spreading throughout Israel and into the southern kingdom of Judah. Idolatry prevailed and real faith languished! Elijah's service would be complete in one day; he had done all he could, yet the Northern Kingdom remained full of unbelief and staggered toward frightful judgment that would occur one hundred and thirty years after Elijah's departure. But Elijah had not failed. And he would not quit. After God called home His one-man army, "the chariot of Israel, and horsemen thereof" (2 Kings 2:12), much labor remained. Elijah lived his last day as a model for Elisha, the sons of the prophets, his nation, and all God's people who desire to make each moment count.

As we read 2 Kings 2:1, we discover the man Elijah standing on the edge of eternity. What enthusiasm was in his step! He would invest his last hours with victorious vision, sharply focused on serving in the key Israelite cities Gilgal, Bethel, and Jericho and passing the mantle of God's law to a desperate nation. Neither sad nor regretful, he knew that God is mightily at work, accomplishing His eternal purposes.

Wouldn't you like to see God work dynamically in your life? Sometimes we read the pages of God's Word and think that men such as Elijah were almost superhuman. After all, he and Enoch are the only two men in the history of mankind who sidestepped death. And Elijah along with Moses appeared with Christ on the Mount of Transfiguration. That is rarefied company! It may be easy to think that because God performed so many miracles through Elijah that his ministry was successful in turning his nation back to God and away from their religiously pluralistic, pagan ways. We can easily and mistakenly suppose that prophets like Elijah were so holy that we can never see God achieve greatness in our lives as He did for them. There is a wonderful verse that tells us otherwise:

> Elias was a man subject to like passions as we are, and he prayed earnestly that it might not rain: and it rained not on the earth by the space of three years and six months. (James 5:17)

Elijah was just like we are, prone to the same temptations and mood swings. He endured physical deprivation (1 Kings 17:1–16), false accusation (1 Kings 18:17), and ministry disappointment (1 Kings 19:1–8). Yet God worked in Elijah's life as he lived each day in God's will. His testimony stirs me as I have spent my ministry years in New York City, our nation's largest megatropolis. We also live in a religiously pluralistic culture. Today, the names have changed but the practices and beliefs have not: over twelve-hundred religions coexist in America. My goal also is to pass on God's eternal truth found in the Word of God to my family, my city, and the people I shepherd. My efforts are often feeble, and my stumbling and failures are many; yet I remain in the race by God's grace, with a burning heart to continue the fight of faith in Jesus Christ to the end.

You don't have to be a pastor or an urban missionary to benefit from this book. Maybe you are a father or mother, a choir member or deacon, a single parent or a single person, an accountant or an engineer, with a heart to be a living sacrifice for God. The central passage of Scripture that we deal with in this book, 2 Kings 2:1–15, will encourage you to live each day as if it were your last, passing on God's truth to a culture that parades unbelief before your eyes. Living each day as Elijah lived his last can infuse our daily routine with the joy of the Lord for which we were made. Living on eternity's edge will help us to be like the apostle Paul and finish our course with joy. It will allow the ministry, which we have received of the Lord Jesus, to testify the gospel of the grace of God (Acts 20:24).

INTRIGUING QUESTIONS

These first fifteen verses of 2 Kings 2 have unusual significance. God performed three spectacular miracles as the mighty prophet Elijah swiftly and uniquely exited earth. His intriguing final movements lead to intriguing questions.

- Why did Elijah go to Bethel, Jericho, and the river Jordan (2 Kings 2:2, 4, 6)?

- Why did Elijah request that Elisha stay behind (2 Kings 2:2, 4, 6)?

- Who were the sons of the prophets and what was their significance (2 Kings 2:3, 5, 7, 15)?

- Why did God miraculously open up the Jordan River on two occasions (2 Kings 2:8, 14)?

- Why did Elisha have to see Elijah depart into heaven (2 Kings 2:10)?

- Why did Elijah leave earth in a whirlwind accompanied by blazing horses and chariots (2 Kings 2:11)?

- Why did Elisha and the sons of the prophets know beforetime of the miracle of Elijah's departure?

- What was the significance of Elijah dropping his mantle upon the ground (2 Kings 2:13)?

- How can we give God's eternal truth to the generation to come?

As you study and meditate on Elijah's last day, discovering the answers to these questions and more, it is my prayer that his testimony will help you make every day count for God, living each day on the edge of eternity. Elijah's heart beat with this passion, and so should ours. You will discover that you have more in common with Elijah than you would ever think.

1 Realizing Life's Brevity . . . On Eternity's Edge

"And it came to pass . . ." (2 Kings 2:1*a*, 9*a*, 11*a*)

A brave Greek soldier had an extremely painful disease that threatened to take his life. Believing he did not have long to live, in each battle he engaged, he willingly went to the frontlines and fought with selfless courage. His looming demise produced a fearlessness in him to face near-death situations. This won his general's admiration, enabling him to see a renowned doctor, which led to his healing. Afterward, the valiant soldier avoided danger and sought to protect his life rather than risk it. His tribulation made him fight well, but his good health destroyed his usefulness as a soldier. What agony gave him, comfort took away! The fire of affliction and the recognition of the brevity and uncertainty of life incited him to heroism.

Similarly, Elijah awoke for his last day on the frontlines of a ferocious war, and self-sacrificing daring pervaded his spirit.

RESILIENT AND READY

God uses an expression throughout Scripture and three times on Elijah's last day on earth that emphasizes the vaporous nature of life. It is the expression "and it came to pass."

God brought many things "to pass" in the dramatic life of Elijah. He overcame drought while hiding from Ahab at the Brook Cherith, but "it came to pass after a while, that the brook dried up" (1 Kings 17:7). He ate from a widow's near-empty barrel in Zarephath and God blessed them; then "it came to pass" that the widow's son fell sick and died (1 Kings 17:17). God shielded Elijah from Ahab's homicidal intentions, but then "it came to pass . . . that the word of the Lord came to Elijah . . . saying, Go, shew thyself unto Ahab; and I will send rain upon the earth" (1 Kings 18:1). Elijah confronted Ahab and eight hundred and fifty false prophets on Mount Carmel (1 Kings 18:19), and many things "came to pass" that day. Most notably, the man of God prayed down fire from heaven and then prayed until it rained, ending years of drought (1 Kings 18:17, 27, 29, 36, 44–45). Soon after this, Elijah wanted to die, being greatly disillusioned. Ahab and Jezebel's idolatry was firmly entrenched in Israel and Elijah was overwhelmed with loneliness. Those dark days quickly came to pass as Elijah recognized God's speaking voice. Elijah stood resilient and ready for the last day of his earthly life. This too would shortly "come to pass" as the horses of fire would be sent from heaven's gate to take Elijah from his brief earthly life.

LIFE IS A LITTLE TIME

Earthly existence. What is it? Life is vapor's time between one's birth and last breath. It is the small dash on one's tombstone. A senior citizen walks to his mailbox, goes into cardiac arrest, and dies instantly. A fit middle-aged father playing basketball jumps to grab a rebound and is dead by the time he hits the ground. A young man returning from the danger of war in Iraq is killed in a car accident on his way home from the airport. A precious life of two months, yet in the womb, mysteriously stops developing and is miscarried. Whether one lives a hundred years or does not live beyond the womb, in light of eternity, life is short.

Life is full of uncertainty, and for many this makes daily existence a meaningless jumble of worthless moments. James asks and answers a mysterious question with amazing simplicity: "For what is your life? It is even a vapour, that appeareth for a little time, and then vanisheth away" (James 4:14). Notice that the two letters in the middle of *life* form the big word *IF*. The word itself reminds us that life is very *iffy*! If we are going to die so soon, what is the point of life at all? What is the reason for sadness and sorrow, pain and pressure? What is the purpose of this brief life? Why are we here and where will we go?

Solomon wrote in Ecclesiastes, "One generation passeth away, and another generation cometh: but the earth abideth forever" (Ecclesiastes 1:4). Intellectually, we know this, but it is natural to trick ourselves to think that our lives will not be as short as others. It is so easy to forget that life is merely a little bit of precarious and unpredictable time that will shortly come to pass. Sooner than we may imagine, we will take our final step, speak our final word, and leave everything behind. We may do it even when least expected.

What would you do with one day left to live? Where would you go? To whom would you speak? What would you pray? Would you shut yourself off from the world and seek solitude? Would you confess your sins? Would you communicate with family, friend, or foe, asking forgiveness and expressing love? Would you tell friends of Christ one final time? Would you be overcome with fear, or would you walk in faith? Would you be full of self-pity or peace? Would you be angry or content?

Would the burning regrets of "what if" or "if only" sear your conscience?

Nearing the end of his brief life, David Brainerd, the great missionary to the Native Americans in the 1740s, wrote the following to a young ministerial student:

> How amazing it is that the living, who know they must die, should, notwithstanding, "put far away the evil day," in a season of health and prosperity, and live at such an awful distance from a familiarity with the grave and the great concerns beyond it! . . . *How rare are the instances of those who live and act from day to day as on the verge of eternity, striving to fill up all their remaining moments in the service and to the honour of their great Master!*[1] (emphasis mine)

Elijah lived on that verge of eternity, showing us how to live there also. Knowing his earthly life would soon end, Elijah filled each moment to honor His Master. Yet Elijah had been living each day as if it were his last for many years.

ELIJAH'S SUDDEN APPEARANCE

We first meet Elijah in 1 Kings 17:1: "And Elijah the Tishbite, who was of the inhabitants of Gilead, said unto Ahab, As the Lord God of Israel liveth, before whom I stand, there shall not be dew nor rain these years, but according to my word." The prophet who would someday ascend into the clouds seemed to drop from them as well, standing before Ahab and predicting that no rain would fall. Previously unknown, this man called the "Tishbite, of the inhabitants of Gilead," suddenly appeared unannounced yet bursting with faith, standing alone before the wicked king. The surname "Tishbite" might refer to his life as a sojourner who was originally from the Galilean town "Tishbe." If this be the case, Elijah was born in Galilee in northern Israel on the west side of the Jordan River, though at the time of the Bible account he lived as a foreigner in Gilead on the east side of Jordan. Gilead means "rocky" and was the rugged, culturally backward territory east of the Jordan River.[2] This mountainous region had been his home, but no more; his sojourn across the Jordan had now taken on a new dimension as he boldly entered Ahab's presence.

Elijah's very name has many things to tell us about God: *El* is the root word for Elohim, or "God." This name reminds us that He is the "Strong One," Who created the entire universe, carving the earth out of nothing but His word.[3] *Jah* is the root for the name Jehovah, or "LORD." This name speaks of God being eternal, immutable, self-existent, and all-sufficient. For the Jew, this high and holy name of God was incomprehensible, unwritable, and unspeakable.[4] This name *Elijah* therefore means "The LORD is God" or "My God is Jehovah." This is significant because Ahab had made Baal worship the official religion in Israel (1 Kings 16:29–34). Elijah lived to challenge these false beliefs and to confront his contemporaries with the truth of the one true God. And Elijah lived up to his name to his very last day. Elijah knew that though his earthly life was fleeting, there is an eternal God, Who gives everlasting life to those who trust in Him.

ELIJAH'S STAND BEFORE GOD

Notice the expression "before whom I stand" (1 Kings 17:1). This phrase reveals the foundation of Elijah's loyal service for God throughout his brief life and his last day. He stood before the Lord fervent in prayer, for he had already prayed that it would not rain and he assertively predicted to Ahab the answer to his plea.[5] He stood gripped with a knowledge of God's Word, realizing that drought was clearly predicted by God as a warning for His people's stubbornness.[6] He stood keenly aware and convicted of the darkness of sin and idolatry that was spreading. Elijah stood absorbed in the glory of the eternal God before him, unfazed by stylish opinions, unimpressed by the popularity of idolatry in Israel (Psalm 16:8–9). Elijah resolutely stood to pass the years of his life as a spiritual pilgrim, abstaining "from fleshly lusts, which war against the soul" (1 Peter 2:11). He stood against Ahab's religiously pluralistic practices, proclaiming to Ahab that God and not Baal was alive, controlling nature. He stood to announce his allegiance to the Lord, refusing to be a mouthpiece for Ahab and Jezebel and their doomed plans, like so many others were (1 Kings 18:19; 22:6). Finally, he stood before God to declare his willingness to labor throughout his life with the label "Ahab's troubler and enemy" (1 Kings 18:17; 21:20). His continuous stand before the living Lord gave him confidence to live for God. The Lord, Who is God, will not be thwarted. First Kings 18:15 reinforces Elijah's constant awareness of the divine presence: "And Elijah said, As the Lord of hosts liveth, before whom I stand, I will surely shew myself unto him to day." While seeing Him Who is invisible, he stood boldly and experienced victory. Forgetting this truth, as he did briefly when he ran in disappointment from Jezebel (1 Kings 19:1–8), he stumbled badly.

Elijah stands as an amazing model for us. It is easy for us to be mechanical in prayer and worship. When was the last time you proclaimed to someone the answer to your prayer right after you prayed but before the answer was evident? Do you pray with an earnest spirit, crying to God with your voice? Have you become callous toward sin? Do you take God's warnings against sin seriously? To Elijah, the Lord was not a vague or subjective idea; He was ultimate reality, Who matters eternally, and the only One Who gives purpose to the uncertainties of life. Elijah was unchanged in his convictions on his last day. He knew that the way to live this brief life that would "come to pass" was to realize moment by moment that we stand before an eternal God, Who has an eternal plan for good.

Miraculously, Elijah's life on earth did not end in death. He ascended in a chariot of fire in his earthly body and entered heaven forever. Though his time on earth ended differently from ours, Elijah's last day contains a reality for us—at the end of our final day we also will live somewhere forever.

Because heaven is a real place, we must not plan merely for time but for eternity. Like the rich fool of Luke 12:13–21, many people are full of plans but empty of time to fulfill those plans. Many plan ahead, but not far enough, "for we must needs die, and are as water spilt on the ground, which cannot be gathered up again" (2 Samuel 14:14). Whatever we are going through today will surely come to pass, and soon our "soul shall be required" of us (Luke 12:20). Like Elijah we need to be faithful unto death.

> **Because heaven is a real place, we must not plan merely for time but for eternity.**

All of us are frail creatures of dust; today we may be as green leaves in the forest's summertime, but soon our autumn will come and we will fade and fall back to the earth. "For all flesh is as grass, and all the glory of man as the flower of grass. The grass withereth, and the flower thereof falleth away: but the word of the Lord endureth for ever" (1 Peter 1:24–25). Jesus Christ died but "death hath no more dominion over him." He Who is the "resurrection and the life" is risen from the dead and ascended to the Father's right hand (John 11:25). He promised to send the Holy Spirit to abide with us forever. He has not left us comfortless but will come to us in the person of the Holy Spirit (John 14:16–18). Now our life is a constant fellowship with Him Who dwells in us. As Jesus Himself lives "unto God" (Romans 6:9–10), so should we. It is appropriate for us therefore to live with a God-centered perspective in the conscious presence of God doing His will because our last day on earth—if we have salvation—will lead to our first day in the presence of the eternal King of Kings!

Reflections for Today

Life is brief, so get busy living "before the Lord." This is crucial for living on eternity's edge. Make a diligent effort to live today as if you may not have another. Depend on God's Spirit and trust in His grace. Demonstrate kindness and patience. Smile at others and speak to them by name. Seek to tell someone of Jesus Christ. An older minister advised Billy Sunday during the early days of his Christian life to spend fifteen minutes a day letting God talk to him through the Scripture, fifteen minutes a day talking to God in prayer, and fifteen minutes talking to someone else about God.[7]

MEMORIZE

James 4:14 "Whereas ye know not what shall be on the morrow. For what is your life? It is even a vapour, that appeareth for a little time, and then vanisheth away."

MEDITATE

Meditate on James 4:13–17.

1. In James 4:13 of what does the one planning take account?

2. In James 4:15 of what does the one planning neglect? How is this more important than the more superficial issues of verse 13?

3. What is evil in James 4:16 and what is sin in James 4:17? Why?

Almighty Lord God,
I praise You that You are strong from everlasting to everlasting. I thank You that You have numbered our days according to Your perfect wisdom. Thank You for the Lord Jesus Christ Who died for me that "he might bring us to God" (1 Peter 3:18). Teach me to live in the light of eternity and allow me to make a difference by Your grace and for Your glory today. In Jesus name, Amen.

2 Experiencing God's Presence ... On Eternity's Edge

"So they went down to Bethel" (2 Kings 2:2*b*)

John Harper possessed a passion for souls. Called of God to preach the gospel in the early 1900s, he pastored churches, conducted evangelistic meetings, and was greatly used by the Lord. When Harper preached at The Moody Church, the members experienced a great sense of God's presence and Harper continued there for three months. "He could not live without souls being won" to Christ.[1] Harper's earnestness was the result of his deep consciousness of God, his love for God's Word, and his desire to seek Him in private prayer.

Because of the blessings of his first visit to The Moody Church, Harper was asked to return in 1912. God would have Harper preach his final sermon in the middle of the Atlantic rather than in America's heartland. On the night of April 14, 1912, as the "unsinkable ship," the *Titanic*, descended into the frigid waters, Harper shouted, "'Let the women, children and the unsaved into the lifeboats.' Harper took his life jacket—the final hope of survival—and gave it to another man."[2] Harper handed his six-year-old daughter to a deck captain with instructions to get her into a lifeboat.

The *Titanic* sank two hours and forty minutes after striking an iceberg. For fifty fearful minutes after that, piercing cries for help filled the dark night as 1,522 drowned. One survivor said, "The sound of people drowning is something I cannot describe to you. And neither can anyone else. It is the most dreadful sound. And there is a dreadful silence that follows it."

During those final minutes, a man drifting on a loose board came within sight of Harper. Struggling in the water, Harper cried to the man, "Are you saved?" "No," the man answered. Harper shouted the words of Acts 16:31: "Believe on the Lord Jesus Christ, and thou shalt be saved." Before responding, the man drifted away into darkness. A few moments later, the current brought them back in sight of each other. Again the dying Harper shouted the question, "Are you saved?" Once again, the man answered, "No." Harper repeated the words from Acts 16:31, the last words anyone heard the preacher say as he slipped into the waters to meet his Savior. The man he sought to win to Christ was saved and when he was brought onto the S.S. *Carpathia*'s lifeboats, he later gave a testimony that he was John Harper's "last convert." Harper spent his final moments the way he lived—on eternity's edge reaching the lost with the message of life. His loyalty even in death was a direct result of his experiencing the presence of God.[3]

THE BIG DEAL ABOUT BETHEL

On Elijah's last day we might wonder, what was the big deal about his going to Bethel? In Scripture and for the nation of Israel, Bethel's significance is great, for it reminded an Israelite living under the Mosaic covenant of the very real and personal presence of God. In Genesis 28, Jacob spent a memorable night there. "He dreamed, and behold a ladder set up on the earth, and the top reached to heaven: and behold the angels of God ascending and descending on it. And, behold, the Lord stood above it, and said, I am the Lord God of Abraham thy father, and the God of Isaac: the land whereon thou liest, to thee will I give it, and to thy seed" (Genesis 28:12–13). There at Bethel, God confirmed the Abrahamic covenant to Jacob: his "seed shall be as the dust of the earth" and "in thy seed shall all the families of the earth be blessed" (Genesis 28:14). Then God promised His presence with a fourth "behold." Genesis 28:15 says, "And, behold, I am with thee, and will keep thee in all places whither thou goest, and will bring thee again into this land; for I will not leave thee, until I have done that which I have spoken to thee of." Jacob awoke, marveling: "Surely the Lord is in this place, and I knew it not, and he was afraid, and said, How dreadful is this place! This is none other but the house of God, and this is the gate of heaven" (Genesis 28:16–17). He called that place Bethel, or "house of God." There at Bethel, Jacob saw things that would forever be etched upon his heart. He saw a ladder and angels and knew that God was intimately involved with the affairs of earth through His ministering servants. He saw the Lord and knew that God would give him that land as an inheritance. Even more vital, in that fourth "behold" it all became personal and real for him. God personally promised Jacob His continuous presence and protection throughout his life. To Jacob, God was not some far-off deity who had done things for his father, Isaac, or grandfather, Abraham. The Lord would do great things for him. Jacob would remain loyal to Him to the day of his death, for God's presence changed the deceiver into a worshiper and prince with God. Scripture tells us that Jacob "when he was a dying, blessed both the sons of Joseph; and worshipped, leaning upon the top of his staff" (Hebrews 11:21). Jacob's Bethel experience was a turning point in his life.

ELIJAH'S TURNING POINT

Elijah also experienced the personal presence of God, directing him to live the rest of his days on eternity's edge. Elijah's turning point came when he heard one little word from God in a still, small voice on Mount Horeb amid gale winds, breaking rocks, shaking mountains, and incinerating fire. After calling fire from heaven (1 Kings 18:30–40), Elijah expected a national revival in Israel. He assumed people would forsake the ways of the false prophets because it was the Lord Who answered by fire. They refused. Not only that, Jezebel was so furious over the slaying of her false prophets that she issued a death warrant for Elijah. In the midst of this great disappointment, Elijah ran from the place of his calling and came to Mount Horeb (1 Kings 19:1–8). There, while mighty chunks of granite tore away from the mountain to blow around like dead leaves, the ground rumbled and swayed under his feet, and the sky blazed with dangerous fire, God spoke to Elijah in a whisper, "Return" (1 Kings 19:15). From that moment Elijah abandoned rudderless living. "Return," God said. And Elijah did. God's voice jolted his conscience, and he returned to reach his sinking nation: he anointed Elisha to fill his place and sought those seven thousand stalwart souls who would not bow their knee to Baal. This became Elijah's delight until the chariots of fire carried him to heaven. According to Scripture, he never wavered after hearing that word.

Have you experienced the reality of God so that your life and service for Christ are a joyful delight? Sometimes we think that the God we read about in the Bible is far away from our daily grind. He isn't! You can experience Him, even today. You too can return to Him if you have run away disappointed or disillusioned. Believe that Christ is risen from the dead and that He has ascended and lives "to make intercession" for us continually. That means He watches out for us and prays for us all the time.

Jesus, as your great High Priest and helper, promises to give you grace to help in time of need. There will never be a moment that He is not with you, caring for you.

> **There will never be a moment that He is not with you, caring for you.**

The fact of Jesus' resurrection does not take Him further away from His followers. In truth it brings Him nearer to us, for His word to Mary after His resurrection, "I ascend unto my Father, and your Father; and to my God, and your God," means that Jesus went to a place of authority but that He will ever be near to us (John 20:17). The ascended Christ is just as near to us as Christ on earth was to the disciples. So read the Word of God with a heart that cries, "My mouth is open, Lord, fill it!" Pray to Him with the passion of the psalmist when he cried, "Hear my cry, O God; attend unto my prayer. From the end of the earth will I cry unto thee, when my heart is overwhelmed: lead me to the rock that is higher than I" (Psalm 61:1–2). Sing to the Lord a new song of praise. Attend a good Bible-believing church with a heart that "fainteth for the courts of the Lord" (Psalm 84:2). He will never leave or forsake us, and we can experience Him just as Jacob or Elijah![4]

BETHEL WAS SINKING

Even though Bethel was a reminder of God's nearness to Jacob, in the days of Elijah Bethel had crashed into an iceberg of trouble. The land was sinking. Bethel was no longer a place where many were loyal to God; in Hosea 10:5 the city is referred to as Beth-aven, or "house of vanity or idolatry," which denotes trouble, sorrow, and pain, particularly lying and treachery. Through idolatry, it had been transformed into a house of deceit and disappointment, of shattered hopes and ultimate destruction because an idol is ineffective to strengthen its followers.[5] How had this happened? After the reign of King Solomon, Israel was divided into two kingdoms, Judah in the south and Israel in the north. Israel's first king, Jeroboam, provoked God to anger by rejecting the truth of God for a false religion that paralleled true worship (1 Kings 12:25–33). Knowing Bethel's great spiritual heritage, Jeroboam reasoned that establishing a worship center there, with impressive idols, feast days, and priests whom he could control, would keep his people from going to Jerusalem. Understanding Jeroboam's false religion is vital to understanding the times of the kings. Of King Omri, one of Jeroboam's successors, the Bible says, "But Omri wrought evil in the eyes of the Lord . . . for he walked in all the way of Jeroboam the son of Nebat, and in his sin wherewith he made Israel to sin, to provoke the Lord God of Israel to anger with their vanities" (1 Kings 16:25–26). The kings that followed Jeroboam are similarly described because Jeroboam's false faith was the essence of evil in the land, ultimately bringing devastation to the Northern Kingdom.

Bethel over time became the city of "the king's chapel, and it [was] the king's court" (Amos 7:13). The word *chapel* means "sanctuary" and signifies Bethel as the king's personal religious shrine. The word *court* speaks of his house. With the king's home and religious life centered there, Bethel became the locus of gross demon worship. Second Chronicles 11:15 states, "And he ordained him priests for the high places, and for the devils, and for the calves which he had made." Jeroboam's message to his citizens appealed to their love of ease: "It is too much for you to go up to Jerusalem: behold thy gods, O Israel, which brought thee up out of the land of Egypt" (1 Kings 12:28). Easily and quickly, God's mighty presence had been replaced by the vain idols of man.

THE ISRAELITES WERE CANAANITES

Although Hosea lived more than one hundred years after Elijah, the prophet's words capture the pervasive unbelief in Israel during both his day and Elijah's last day. Like Elijah, Hosea was a prophet to the Northern Kingdom of Israel. He reminded the people of God that Jacob "had power over the angel, and prevailed: he wept, and made supplication unto him: he found him in Bethel, and there he spake with us" (Hosea 12:4). Hosea references two tremendous moments in Jacob's life. First he recalls the night Jacob wrestled alone with God until the breaking of the day, pleading and prevailing, "I will not let thee go, except thou bless me" (Genesis 32:26). That also was the night God changed Jacob's name to Israel. Next Hosea evokes Jacob's return to Bethel to build an altar (Genesis 35:1–15). There God "appeared unto Jacob again . . . and blessed him," reminding him that his name should not be called Jacob, "but Israel shall be thy name" (Genesis 35:9–10). Israel—a prince with God!

Speaking specifically of the Northern Kingdom, Israel, Hosea refers to the once princely descendants of Jacob with the expression, "He is a merchant" (Hosea 12:7). The Hebrew word translated *merchant* here appears eighty-nine times in our King James Version as "Canaan." God thunders against His people, "Canaanites!" How unlike their ancestor Jacob the wicked

Israelites had become! This "abrupt and contemptuous word, 'merchant,' demonstrated a vast contrast to their God-given name, 'Israel.'"[6] As the mouthpiece of God Hosea proclaims, "He is a merchant, the balances of deceit are in his hand: he loveth to oppress. And Ephraim said, Yet I am become rich, I have found me out substance: in all my labours they shall find none iniquity in me that were sin" (Hosea 12:7–8). "Ephraim" is another name for the Northern Kingdom because Ephraim was the largest and most influential tribe of Israel.

Like the polytheistic nations surrounding them, Israel wrongly assumed that material prosperity equaled God's blessing. They adopted the business practices of the Canaanites, sought profit through pragmatic methods, and drove hard bargains. They valued gain above God. Self-righteousness coupled with their greed as they sensed no shame in any of their deceitful labor. Spiritually, they were blind and proud.[7] No longer "princes with God," the merchandising Israelites became like covetous Canaanites. Unlike Jacob of old, they refused to wrestle with God in prevailing prayer. They ceased hungering for God's blessing. And they stopped experiencing God's presence (Genesis 32:26). The people of Bethel in both Hosea's and Elijah's day had forsaken God to chase the winds of insignificance. This is the city that Elijah went to on his last day!

Elijah's goal as a prophet was to restore the people to a place of experiencing God so that they could glorify Him and live loyally to Him, finding satisfaction in His ever-present help. One cannot go where God is not, but one can go where men have forgotten Him. God's omnipresence does not guarantee that He will be experienced equally by everyone. Bethel on Elijah's last day was a city of scoffers who had forsaken God (2 Kings 2:23).

WHERE ARE OUR BETHELS?

Counterfeit forms of Christianity prevail in our seemingly impregnable nation, and in New York City, my chosen mission field. Both are sinking. In the 1850s a layman named Jeremiah Lanphier began a noonday prayer meeting in New York City. Only six showed up that first day, but in the weeks that followed, more came as God's presence was experienced mightily! Prayer meetings seeking God spread throughout the city, then radiated across the nation—and even the ocean—as revival broke out in various places around the world. Incredibly, the last real revival America experienced began in New York City at high noon![8]

Less than seventy years later, in 1922, Harry Emerson Fosdick, the liberal minister of the infamous Riverside Church in New York City, preached one of the most famous sermons in American history entitled "Shall the Fundamentalists Win?"[9] Fundamentalists did lose the battle for the denominations, the seminaries, and the churches, and those who stood for the fundamentals of the faith properly separated from the widespread rejection of clear doctrinal truth prevailing in the major denominations.[10] Sadly, however, fundamentalists began a steady flight from the cities that needed the very good news they had. In the vacuum, theological liberalism took deep root in our cities while many Bible-believing Christians and their churches moved to the suburbs and rural areas.

In 1969, the Stonewall Inn was a gay bar in the heart of Greenwich Village that stayed in business by bribing the police. It was then illegal for gays to openly gather in taverns. On June 28, 1969, the sodomite patrons rebelled against the police and barricaded the officers inside the inn. Crowds taunted them from outside. This event was a landmark victory for the budding Gay Rights movement, for it garnered sympathetic media coverage. To celebrate the Stonewall Inn Riot, June continues to be "Gay Pride" month.

It is now common for mainline denominational churches to condone homosexuality as a God-pleasing lifestyle. In 2003 the Episcopal Church in America approved an openly sodomite bishop named Gene Robinson to lead Episcopalians in New Hampshire. Speaking in favor of Robinson, an Episcopal bishop stated, "We have a wonderful evangelistic tool to strengthen the life of the church."[11] Here, much like in Jeroboam's Bethel, convenience is valued more highly than scriptural obedience, and God's Word is abandoned for carnal delights. For these leaders, "evangelism" has nothing to do with the death, burial, and resurrection of Christ, the salvation of souls, the regeneration of the Holy Spirit, or faith in the finished work and perfect righteousness of Christ. Evangelism has become pragmatism, a scheme that can increase church attendance and offerings and seeks to win people to moral relativism and religious pluralism! These attitudes characterize a culture that has been given up by God (Romans 1:18–32). Just as God condemned the Israelites as Canaanites, He will condemn religious leaders who turn Christianity into pragmatism.

What should be done? Do we move further away from our cities and ethnic multitudes like Elijah when he ran from Jezebel's wrath? Do we turn away from our cities in frustration and fear because of a scarcity of true conversion? Or, ought we to suffer shame for Christ in our own Bethels? God has much people in the city, and there are still those who have not bowed to unbelief. God's encouraging words spoken to Elijah at Mount Horeb are repeated in the New Testament to give us a passion for Jews in particular, but for all souls in general. When we feel alone in our ministry and fruit seems sporadic, God still says, "I have reserved to myself seven thousand men, who have not bowed the knee to the image of Baal. Even so then at this present time also there is a remnant according to the election of grace" (Romans 11:4–5).[12] Heed the call of God and go, fearlessly facing the hazards. But first we must truly experience God and know that He is with us. We must personally know that the Lord Jesus Christ is risen from the dead to be our ever-present help. We must not become like "Canaanites" because our lifestyle is to be "without covetousness . . . for he hath said, I will never leave thee, nor forsake thee. So that we may boldly say, The Lord is my helper, and I will not fear what man shall do unto me" (Hebrews 13:5–6). We too have God's promise to pass on, and it is still right to risk our lives for Christ and to live loyally for God and His truth on eternity's edge!

REFLECTION FOR TODAY
Experiencing the reality of God through the promises of Scripture is necessary to living true to God on eternity's edge. Make time to experience God. Have you met God and personally experienced Him?

MEMORIZE
2 Timothy 4:7 "I have fought a good fight, I have finished my course, I have kept the faith."

MEDITATE

Meditate on 2 Timothy 4. These are Paul's final words on eternity's edge before his martyrdom. God's presence was real to him in awful circumstances as he wrote his final letter. Paul remained faithful unto death.

1. What was Paul's command to Timothy in 2 Timothy 4:1–5 on how to serve in the idol-laden city of Ephesus (a city like Bethel in the days of Elijah)?

2. What are some of the reasons Paul could have experienced loneliness in his final days in prison (vv. 9–10, 14–16)?

3. What was the remedy for potential loneliness in that circumstance (vv. 9, 11, 13, 16–19)?

4. Describe Paul's confidence of God's presence with him in a lonely prison (vv. 16–19).

Lord of heaven and earth,
I long to experience You in spirit and truth! Thank You that You are with me to strengthen me today. Grant me boldness not to be ashamed of Your gospel even in places like Bethel. May I be faithful to You and Your truth because "great is thy faithfulness" to me (Lamentations 3:23). I realize there is a battle for truth so help me to compassionately contend for the faith You have given to us. In Jesus' name, Amen.

3 Remembering God's Power . . . On Eternity's Edge

"So they came to Jericho" (2 Kings 2:4*b*)

Jericho is linked to the first day and the last day of Elijah's ministry. When we hear the name "Jericho," images arise of Joshua and the Israelites, of blowing trumpets, of shouting voices, and of tumbling walls as God judged the ungodly and wonderfully saved Rahab and her family. Most of all, Jericho reminds us of God's power. Without missile or machine gun, God prevailed to flatten the stout walls and deliver His people in the earlier days of Israel's history. More than five hundred years later, God's miraculous might appears to have been forgotten in Jericho during Ahab's reign; he had tried to delete that memory of God's wrath and mercy. The people trusted in another false deity, Baal, and Jericho was a central city for Baal worship during Ahab's rule.

JERICHO: A STRATEGIC GATEWAY

Elijah's sudden appearance in the biblical record occurred just after Ahab rebuilt Jericho's walls. What a defiant act that was! Ahab ignored God's bone-chilling curse to anyone who rebuilt those walls: "And Joshua adjured them at that time, saying, Cursed be the man before the Lord, that riseth up and buildeth this city

Jericho: he shall lay the foundation thereof in his firstborn, and in his youngest son shall he set up the gates of it" (Joshua 6:26). This defiant act exemplified Ahab's evil and cemented his loyalty to his wife and her heathen deity Baal. Baal worship motivated Ahab to allow the perverse sacrifice of the contractor's oldest and youngest sons; they were buried in the walls to appease that false god (1 Kings 16:29–17:1).[1] This awful deed resulted in Elijah's predicting drought upon the land (1 Kings 17:1). The true prophets of God were marked for death and had to hide in order to preserve their lives (1 Kings 18:3–4, 13).

Jericho's location as a border city made it a strategic gateway into the Northern Kingdom. Located immediately west of the Jordan River, it was reasonable to believe that a walled Jericho would protect Israel from invading nations. Strengthening Jericho made political sense for Ahab, but it highlighted his pride and unbelief. God could well defend Israel without fortification, and He yearned for His people to know that He was their fortress, their deliverer, and their high tower (Psalm 18:2).

Jericho's position close to the King's Highway, which stretched from Egypt in the south to Damascus in the north, potentially made it a major economic center for trade. I can imagine Ahab dreaming of a strong Jericho, controlling trade routes and fulfilling its role as the doorway into the heartland of Israel. Ahab hoped that a well-built Jericho would enrich his kingdom, assist in making his name great among men, and trivialize the God of Elijah. Ahab hoped that Baal would help him accomplish these goals.

When you hear of Baal, do not think of some long-ago faith to which we cannot relate. Baal worshipers would fit well into the thinking of today's religious pluralists. This falsehood was obsessed with the environment, worshiping the creation above the

Creator. In 1 Kings 17:1, Elijah was not giving Ahab a weather report when he said, "There shall not be dew nor rain these years, but according to my word," but was challenging the false god of Ahab with the truth. The Lord not Baal was sovereign over nature. Ahab trusted that Baal, the god of the sun, land, thunder, lightning, and rain would prosper his nation economically. A healthy economy was of utmost importance for those who bowed before Baal, and they readily sacrificed their children for the overall good of the nation either by burying them in the impressive, new walls of Jericho or by causing them to be sacrificed by fire (2 Chronicles 33:6). For Baal worshipers, life was cheap, akin to the thinking of modern-day "pro-choice" supporters. Finally, Baal worship was consumed with moral relativism, immoral perversions, and humanism. The religion was popular because its pleasure-driven creed tolerated nearly everything but truth.

> **When you hear of Baal, do not think of some long-ago faith to which we cannot relate.**

Although Israel did not acknowledge it, Baal worship was exceedingly dangerous to their national life. It was deceptive because those practicing it maintained a superficial belief in the true God that had little to no impact on their daily lives. In Jeremiah's day, Baal worship had spread into Jerusalem and into the temple, yet the people were ignorant of its dangerous advance. God pleaded with His people that had forsaken Him for falsehood: "How canst thou say, I am not polluted, I have not gone after Baalim?" (Jeremiah 2:23). "Yet thou sayest, Because I am innocent, surely his anger shall turn from me. Behold, I will plead with thee, because thou sayest, I have not sinned" (Jeremiah 2:35). When it came to the nonnegotiable absolute of the law of God, Baal worship sought silently to establish itself as a parallel faith, slowly usurping and then ultimately replacing true worship. In summary, Baal worship was pro-choice environmentalism that craved a strong economy, pursued any pleasure, and tolerated any religion that would peacefully coexist alongside it. It sounds like American pop culture in the twenty-first century!

Of all places to go, on the last day of his life, Elijah entered into this stronghold of false worship to encourage the sons of the prophets who would not bow to the chief deity of Jericho. He went believing God had more souls like Rahab to graciously redeem, knowing God was still at work, for a "remnant according to the election of grace" lived in Jericho (Romans 11:5). His steps were energized because God had judged Ahab's house according to His faithful word (1 Kings 21:17–29). By this time Ahab had died as had his son, King Ahaziah, who had sought Baal for healing from disease (2 Kings 1).[2] Elijah saw Jericho as a spiritually strategic outpost in the battle to reach those who would not bow to Baal. Ahab could rebuild walls, but he could not erase God from the minds and hearts of all Israel. It is impossible to know what Elijah said in Jericho, but I can envision Elijah passionately seeking to write the power of God's name back onto the blackboard of Jericho's forgotten history. I imagine Elijah challenging the inhabitants of Jericho with this fact: "God will protect and prosper Jericho all by Himself! Do not put your faith in these new walls or a growing economy, but trust in God's power!" Perhaps Elijah preached the fitting words of David from Psalm 62:

> Ahab was a tottering fence who sought to cast God down from His excellency! He delighted in lies. Our king seemed religious as he blessed with his mouth, but inwardly he cursed God and sold himself "to work wick-

edness in the sight of the Lord" (1 Kings 21:25). If you put him in the balance, he was "altogether lighter than vanity." Now he is dead and so is his son! "Trust not in his oppression . . . and if riches increase, set not your heart upon them. God has spoken once; twice have I heard this; that power belongs unto God!" (Psalm 62:9–11)

Elijah understood that he was not wasting his time by calling people to remember that the Lord God omnipotent rules over the kingdoms of men.

SAVED BUT NOT DEDICATED

In our culture so inundated with moral relativism mirroring Baal worship, God can easily be forgotten. Many declare faith in Christ but live superficially for him. Joe had been saved as a fifteen-year-old on the streets of Williamsburg, Brooklyn, but he never found a church in which to grow spiritually. Years passed, the joy of the Lord faded, and Joe forgot to seek first the Lord, His kingdom, and His righteousness. He went into the army, went to college, and later married Juanita. Although a void gnawed within his soul, he did not know where to go. The eyes of God were upon him, however, as he commuted to work each day in the New York City subways.

That is where he saw Carmine, an old friend from his neighborhood. A faithful Christian in our Manhattan church, Carmine began sharing with Joe the truth of God's Word and salvation, but Joe told him that he already knew the Lord as His Savior. Carmine then invited him to our church, but Joe did not come. Occasionally over the course of a year, they would meet on the train and the conversation always turned toward the Word of God. Carmine was not sure of Joe's interest and actually thought that Joe tried to avoid him. But Carmine persisted nonetheless as God's still small voice to his childhood companion. He shared gospel tracts and church brochures, not knowing if there would be any fruit. Unknown to Carmine, the Holy Spirit had begun to draw Joe as spiritual hunger in his heart grew. Joe later told me, "I knew I needed to dedicate myself to the Lord. I tried everything this world has to offer, but nothing satisfied. I knew I needed to come to your church to re-dedicate my life to Christ." His very first Sunday he did just that.

Soon after, Joe's wife came to church with him. Although not a Christian, Juanita listened attentively with an open heart. My wife, Debbie, gave her the entire gospel in a personal discussion after a service. Around the same time, someone on the street gave Juanita a gospel tract. She went home and read it, and the words from Scripture sank into her heart. Miraculously, she was born again. She called Debbie and me that day, telling us the good news! Joe and Juanita followed the Lord in believer's baptism and continue to grow in His grace.

SAVED ON SEPTEMBER 11, 2001

Chris finally knew on 9/11 that he had to surrender control to the Lord. His brother Dave had been saved in 1993 and shortly after that Chris went away to college. Chris told me,

> I thought born-again Christians were crazy because of how they were portrayed by the media. My brother bought me a Bible and over the next few years I took it with me wherever I moved, but strangely I never read it. When my brother started praying for me, the next semester at school my roommates were all Christians. I thought it weird, but I attributed it to my brother's prayers. He continued witnessing to me.

The week before September 11, 2001, I went to a wedding. I got as drunk as I could, but my brother had given me some salvation sermons which I reluctantly listened to on the way home. On 9/11 I called Dave, and he put the events of that day in a biblical perspective. I knew that if God was not in control, there could be a 9/11 every day! I also knew that I could die at any moment, so that night I asked God to take control of my life and I believed in Jesus Christ. I became a new person with new desires. I finally started to read the Bible Dave had given me years before, and God started speaking to my heart. A month later I began to go to church. I threw out my liquor and my music and I have been following the Lord ever since.

Chris now assists in our Heritage of Faith radio program, organizes church activities, and leads a men's adult Bible fellowship class. In our modern day Jericho, God is at work!

Elijah's ministry challenges us to stand for God in influential places and key cities that have forgotten His power. People like Joe and Juanita and Chris are all around us. Man is a master at forgetting, so we must ever put people in remembrance of eternal truth: the power of God's Word, the glory of God's Son, and the comfort of God's Spirit. Elijah's excursion into Jericho motivates us to serve where results seem scarce and few are saved. We labor knowing that He is at work in the hearts of men, and if He sends us we must go.

REFLECTIONS FOR TODAY

Remember God's power is for the glory of God as we live on eternity's edge. Make time to pray today for those loved ones who are not saved. Ask God to plant a great burden for souls in your heart. Pray also for missionaries in difficult places that God would save precious lives for His glory. Do not give up seeking to win the lost to salvation in Christ.

MEMORIZE

Psalm 62:8 "Trust in him at all times; ye people, pour out your heart before him: God is a refuge for us."

MEDITATE

Meditate on Psalm 62 and consider how only God can provide stillness, salvation, and strength to your soul.

1. In Psalm 62:1–4, what does the psalmist recognize about God?

2. In verses 5–8, what does it mean to have our "expectation" (v. 5) upon God and to "pour out your heart before him" (v. 8)?

3. According to verses 9–12, what belongs to God?

Dear God of power,
My soul waits on You. I praise You that You are a great God of salvation "who will have all men to be saved, and to come unto the knowledge of the truth" (1 Timothy 2:4). May I not fear to proclaim Your name in those places where You have been forgotten. Give me a vision today to boldly evangelize those who are lost! In Jesus' name, Amen.

4 Warring Relentlessly . . . On Eternity's Edge

"And they stood by Jordan . . . and . . . the waters . . .
were divided hither and thither, so that they two
went over on dry ground" (2 Kings 2:7b–8b)

God is a "man of war," and virtually every book of the Bible tells us of God's warring activity (Exodus 15:3). It is not strange therefore to conclude that God divided the waters of Jordan on Elijah's last day to show His people their daily involvement in genuine spiritual conflict. After comparing the four times in Scripture that God miraculously opened up rivers, I have concluded that God transformed raging waters into dry passage ground to reveal His glorious might to triumph over any crisis or enemy in a time of war.[1] This bona fide battle was between God and Satan, truth and error. The prophets of Baal and the priest's of Jeroboam's idolatry were on the side of Satan and error. Elijah, Elisha, and the sons of the prophets were on the side of God and truth. That sounds dogmatic and absolute, cut and dried. It is. The true Word of God was at the heart of this war as Elijah sought to reestablish the testimony of God in the hearts of the religiously pluralistic urban centers of Bethel and Jericho. Bethel, the hub of Jeroboam's counterfeit

Judaism, and Jericho, a center for Baal worship, were frontline cities in God's assault. The schools of the prophets led by Elijah in those cities were the training centers for God's combatants, and the Jordan River opened on Elijah's last day to signify to those young preachers that God would be victorious ultimately in the conflict.

It's Cut and Dried: God Wins

The two other river openings in Scripture during the days of Moses and Joshua strengthen the view that river openings emphasize the reality of war. When Moses stood at the Red Sea, war breathed down Israel's back as they fled from Egypt (Exodus 14:10–31). Pharaoh and the world's most impressive army "marched after" Israel and caused them to freeze with fear (Exodus 14:10). As God said simply, "Go forward," He opened the Red Sea to deliver Moses and his people from Pharaoh's militia of "horses, his chariots, and his horsemen" (Exodus 14:15, 23). God triumphed, burying Pharaoh's armed forces in the sea, and the result was immediate: Israel "feared the Lord, and believed the Lord, and his servant Moses" (Exodus 14:31). The enemy that sank into the Red Sea as a stone was an everlasting reminder to God's people that He is great and there is none to be feared and served as He. Moses sang out: "The Lord is a man of war: the Lord is his name" (Exodus 15:3). It was war and God won.

When Joshua stood at the Jordan River, there was war ahead of Israel, and God opened up the Jordan River to assure His chosen that He would conquer all the enemy nations that populated the Promised Land. Joshua had told them, "Hereby ye shall know that the living God is among you, and that he will without fail drive out from before you the Canaanites, and the

Hittites, and the Hivites, and the Perizzites, and the Girgashites, and the Amorites, and the Jebusites" (Joshua 3:10). The relatively tiny nation that passed through the Jordan River on dry ground was "prepared for war" and ready for "battle" (Joshua 4:13). Something fascinating was buried underneath the waters of Jordan—not soldiers and chariots, but stones: "Joshua set up twelve stones in the midst of Jordan, in the place where the feet of the priests which bare the ark of the covenant stood" (Joshua 4:9). The stones were a memorial of God's unstoppable power to overwhelm the strong enemies within walled cities in the ensuing battles. Nothing—not overflowing rivers or giant adversaries—could stop Israel's victorious advance. On the other side of the Jordan River, just before the battle of Jericho, Joshua met a soldier with a drawn sword. This soldier was worthy of worship; He was the preincarnate Lord Jesus Christ, the captain of the Lord's angel armies. Fighting the battles in the heavenly places, He reminds us that God is a warrior (Joshua 5:13–15).[2]

SPIRITUAL WARFARE SWIRLS ALL AROUND

In 2 Kings, the Jordan River opened to reinforce the reality of unavoidable spiritual warfare swirling around Elijah, Elisha, and the sons of the prophets. This warfare could not be postponed. No army sought their physical destruction, but a spiritual battle raged in the land to destroy the truth of God's Word from human hearts. God opened the river for that two-man army of Elijah and Elisha, showing the importance of their spiritual battle to establish God's law in the land and for that generation to tear down the errors of false worship rooted firmly in Jericho and in Bethel. The young prophets knew that Elijah was departing that day, but they did not know that they were about to witness a miracle. God had more of Himself to reveal as they followed His steps. When the fifty young prophets saw Elijah and Elisha pierce the river on dry ground, they knew deep within their soul that God was with them just as He had been in the days of Moses and Joshua. A lasting impression of God's warring strength was demonstrated to them. We do not know how many miracles these young men had seen, but this one indelibly impacted them to carry God's Word throughout their land. They knew their God was "glorious in his apparel, travelling in the greatness of strength" (Isaiah 63:1). It was nothing for God to defeat the ungodly forces arrayed against them. They too must learn to fear and believe in the Lord and respect the leadership of his servants Elijah and Elisha. They knew there was a great cause for them to set their hope in God, not forget His works, and keep his commandments until their last day.

GOD'S HAND IS STILL MIGHTY

Opening the river helped Elisha and the sons of the prophets see that "with God all things are possible" (Matthew 19:26). After the opening of the Rea Sea, Moses praised God for His power: "Thy right hand, O Lord, is become glorious in power: thy right hand, O Lord, hath dashed in pieces the enemy. . . . Who is like thee, glorious in holiness, fearful in praises, doing wonders?" (Exodus 15:6, 11*b*). Facing an uncharted desert with two million men, women, and children, Israel needed to believe that God could do the impossible. When God split apart the Jordan River, Joshua honored God by saying, "For the Lord your God dried up the waters of Jordan from before you, until ye were passed over, as the Lord your God did to the Red sea, which he dried up from before us, until we were gone over: that all the people of the earth might know the hand of the Lord, that it is mighty: they ye might fear the Lord your God for ever" (Joshua 4:23–24). God cleaves rivers so that His people and the nations will know His omnipotence. Elijah, Elisha, and the sons of the prophets could "go forward," knowing that God's mighty hand was sufficient for their battle. There was still a battle for the cities like Bethel and Jericho. Impregnable walls of false worship had been built, and God had a remnant there that refused to bow to error. The schools of the prophets continued warring and growing, fearlessly proclaiming God's absolute truth to that religiously pluralistic land.

LOCKED IN DAILY BATTLE

We also are locked in a daily struggle, wrestling against spiritual wickedness in high places. Life is war and we must fight the good fight to our very last step.[3] We need not freeze in fear before our river of impossibility. We can press on to the mark of our high calling of God in Christ Jesus, serving God and others for His glory. Our prayerful communication with God should not be like using a "domestic intercom to call upstairs for more comforts in the den." Rather, prayer is a wartime walkie-talkie linking us with our Commander in heaven so that we receive the needed power in our battle and He in turn gets the glory.[4]

Sadly, casualties of this warfare litter the battlefield. Divorce, abuse, illicit sex, gambling, and drugs destroy homes and lives daily.

> Life is war and we must fight the good fight to our very last step.

We often forget the incredible battle we are in. Do we merely pray for increased comforts in our already cozy dens because we don't have high-definition television with surround-sound speakers? Do we feel discontent because we can't afford the latest electronic gadget or clothing fashion? Are we blasé in our attitude toward the weapons of our warfare: the Scripture, prayer, His church, the ordinances, and holy living? It is time for us to reject contentment with worldliness and recover the meaning of "godliness with contentment is great gain" (1 Timothy 6:6). A wartime mentality must take hold of our soul; superficial spirituality must be renounced!

HOSTILITY IN THE HOME

My wife often reminds me that there is an intense spiritual battle being waged against our home and marriage. Sadly, the battlefield is sometimes the kitchen and the enemy appears to be other members of the household; either the children fight with one another, or my wife and I find ourselves in conflict with them. Is it too much to confess that sometimes my wife and I draw swords against each other? A reality we often forget in the daily struggle against the Devil is this: "We wrestle not against flesh and blood, but against principalities, against powers, against the rulers of the darkness of this world, against spiritual wickedness in high places" (Ephesians 6:12). The real enemy is Satan, the accuser of the brethren, and when we give in to his temptation and deception, we can easily begin fighting against those we love and should be fighting with (Revelation 12:10).

I remember having a disagreement with Debbie, and afterward it seemed like a river of impossibility to restore the joy and feelings of love in our relationship. This is hard to admit as a church planter and pastor, but I was struggling in my marriage. During this time, I discovered a book entitled *If Only He Knew: What No Woman Can Resist* by Gary Smalley. That sounded like something I definitely needed, so I began reading because I was desperate. Immediately, the Lord began dealing with my pride and failure to meet my wife's needs and to understand her heart as a woman. But when I got to page 80, something convicted me to my soul's depth that brought me to my knees in repentance before God. Smalley writes, "If a couple has been married for more than five years, any persistent disharmony in their marriage relationship is usually attributable to the husband's lack of understanding and applying genuine love."[5] I could not refute that statement as I considered the way I often treated my precious partner. I spoke to Debbie about what I was reading and humbled myself before God and her to take responsibility for the friction in our home. What joy and fellowship we experienced when I expressed genuine sorrow to my wife in the areas where I offended her! There have certainly been other conflicts since that one, but crossing that river of impossibility by humbling myself has given me confidence that God can deliver us in any hostility we face in our home.

THE GOD OF DRY GROUND AT HIGH TIDE

There is a battle to fight in modern urban centers similar to Bethel and Jericho of old. We continually battle with the flesh, which the world system tempts with pride and pleasures for the eyes and body. The Devil casts his fiery darts of doubt and discouragement. We struggle and sometimes fail to do and say the right thing at the right time. We often fail to pray and sometimes faint. There is a strain to maintain love and fellowship in a marriage or to lead one's family to make spiritual decisions. There is a war to keep morally pure in a sex-addicted culture. Can a Christian truly retain sexual purity today? Is premarital sex unavoidable? Are all marriages doomed to end in divorce? No! The fear of the Lord leads us to see that God can split open impossible rivers we face as we follow in His steps.

It is a war to win souls to Christ, to build them in the faith, and to establish them in the church. It is tough to start churches in a modern Babylon, where Scripture is scorned. Every day presents a new river of difficulty that may seem impossible to cross in our human strength. But by the power of the risen Christ we are "more than conquerors through him that loved us" (Romans 8:37). The same God Who opened up rivers can open up hearts and open up great doors of opportunity in our places of service.

> **The same God Who opened up rivers can open up hearts.**

Rather than focusing on what is impossible, we can attempt with faith and sacrificial abandon that which can astonish the world. We hunger to live pure, to evangelize, to study the Word of God, to start churches, and to go to the mission field. Why? Nothing is impossible with God. We conquer temptation, overcome habits, and change into the image of Jesus Christ by the power of His Holy Spirit and His grace. God's hand is still mighty; He is the God of "dry ground" at high tide.

SUNBATHERS AND FALSE ACCUSERS

In New York City church planting I regularly encounter the "Jordan River" of difficulty. Recently, during one of our sweltering summer days, I left church after a Sunday service and walked into a nearby park to see it full of sunbathers. Right in the middle of Manhattan! It seemed young people bearing God's image were more desirous of sitting in the sun than sitting at Jesus' feet. I groaned in my soul, for it seems humanly impossible to break through the impregnable walls of indulgence and God-forgetfulness. Nevertheless, God's promises motivate me to press on, for He is with me and has "much people in this city" (Acts 18:10).

At a church I had established and pastored, I was falsely accused of seeking to purchase a building in my name. This caused turmoil in my heart and trouble for our church. I wondered how the dear people I had sacrificed for and given myself to could actually think that I would want to betray them and steal from them. But God comforted me through His Word: "As sorrowful, yet always rejoicing; as poor, yet making many rich; as having nothing, and yet possessing all things" (2 Corinthians 6:10). That accusation proved untrue and that church bought a building and continues to this day, proclaiming God's Word in the Queens community.

REHOBOTH

On a Wednesday afternoon my wife called me while I was driving home: "I have good news and bad news. I will tell you the good news first. The Lord is going to provide a wonderful place for us to meet this Sunday." The bad news was clear: we were being asked to leave the public school space that our church rented. Debbie continued, "Tom, the custodial head of the public school we rent just called to tell me the New York City Board of Education will not allow us to meet at the school again. We will have to find another meeting place by this Sunday."

Stunned, I wondered, "How can we find a suitable place to meet and tell our entire church in four days? This will be impossible!" I went home and prayed. I e-mailed some friends, "Pray!" Then God gave me a verse. In Genesis 26 the Philistines kept stealing Isaac's wells, until he dug one and called it Rehoboth. He said, "For now the Lord hath made room for us, and we shall be fruitful in the land" (Genesis 26:22*b*). I believed God would make room for us somewhere so that we could bring forth fruit for His glory. The battle was His. The next day the Lord led me to the Village Community School, a private school in the heart of Greenwich Village. In fifteen minutes we secured a better meeting place for less money than the one we had previously had. God made room for us by His promise through prayer. That weekend a man in our church made a banner that read "Rehoboth Sunday" to celebrate God's faithfulness to us. God has exceeding great and precious promises for every Jordan River problem we face![6]

PATHWAYS THROUGH IMPOSSIBLE RIVERS

Maybe you are facing a great problem in your life and you need to find a pathway through a river of impossibility. Every day puts us into a new trench of spiritual conflict. Satan continually attacks God and His people. Paul experienced a "messenger of Satan to buffet" him (2 Corinthians 12:7). The word *buffet* means literally to beat and pummel someone black and blue. Satan pounds us with wicked and accusing thoughts. His goal is to snatch God's Word out of our hearts. He kindles and casts darts of overwhelming desires at our heart: ambition, greed, or sexual craving. There is a war for our personal holiness and sexual purity, for our children, and for our marriages. Seek God until you find Him! "Trust in the Lord with all thine heart" (Proverbs 3:5). "Fear God, and keep his commandments: for this is the whole duty of man" (Ecclesiastes 12:13*b*). Do not allow the mighty weapon of prayer to grow rusty. Remember that we wrestle against mighty spiritual forces of wickedness (Ephesians 6:12). Sustaining a daily devotional time is never easy, but we will be burned by Satan if we don't! Daily claim the cleansing through Christ's blood and delight in the truth found in God's Word. Open up your heart to God. On your knees. While you drive. While you jog, memorize a verse and pray. Write down a verse in a notebook; meditate on it through the day. Connect with God's heart. Possibly you are embarking upon a new ministry and you need God to open up the way. Are you teaching a new class, taking on a new office of deacon, or assuming the leadership of a new church? Are you beginning a new marriage or are you a new parent? Are you beginning a new course of study or starting a new job? Do you wonder if you can do it? Are you afraid of really blowing it? Claim a promise of God until it becomes your very own! He is with you to fight for you and with you. With God's sword, you can confidently fight the good fight of faith, confronting and conquering every problem while living on eternity's edge.

REFLECTIONS FOR TODAY

Spiritual warfare is relentless and battles must be fought on eternity's edge. Make a promise from God your very own. Claim God's promise at the river of impossibility. Do not wait until you are on the victory side of the river to sing the song of victory. Praise God with the promise facing the insurmountable problem.

MEMORIZE

Ephesians 6:16 "Above all, taking the shield of faith, wherewith ye shall be able to quench all the fiery darts of the wicked."

MEDITATE

Meditate on Ephesians 6:10–18. This passage tells us that we are in a great warfare that often causes us tremendous problems in our flesh. Purpose today to stand with the entire spiritual armor described by Paul. Which piece have you laid aside? Ask God for His strength to be a weapon of righteousness as you stand for Him on eternity's edge (Romans 6:13).

1. In Ephesians 6:11–13, who is our real enemy and how are we to withstand him?

2. In verses 14–17, how can the aspects of God's armor protect you from many potential problems?

3. Which piece have you neglected recently and what can you do to change?

4. According to verse 18, how does prayer relate to the entire passage of taking on this armor? How can prayer assist you in overcoming great problems in your life?

Dear victorious Lord,
I praise You that You are a Man of war, strong and
mighty in battle! You are the King of glory, Who will fight
for me today! I praise You that Your right hand is mighty
and strong today for all the problems I face. I trust You
today to confront any battle and overcome any obstacle.
I realize anew that life is war, so arm me with the whole
armor today that I may stand in Your strength against all
of the strategies of Satan and be more than a conqueror
through Christ Who loves me. In Jesus' name, Amen.

5 Following God's Direction . . . On Eternity's Edge

"The Lord hath sent me . . . " (2 Kings 2:2*b*, 4*b*, 6*b*)

Elijah awoke on his final day with clear directives from God. On three separate occasions he said to Elisha, "The Lord hath sent me." First the Lord sent him to Bethel. Then he said, "The Lord hath sent me to Jericho" (2 Kings 2:4). Finally, he announced, "The Lord hath sent me to Jordan" (2:6). We have seen the significance of these three stops on Elijah's last day. Now, let's focus on the response of Elijah and his disciple Elisha to follow God's will immediately and exactly. With uncompromising zeal, Elijah knew that the last day of his life was not the time to disobey. The phrase "the Lord hath sent me" is a successful maxim by which to live each day on eternity's edge. It shows that God has a will for our daily life, and His will comes to us from His heart as an expression of His love. Just as the Lord sent Elijah, so He can send you. Will your daily steps have greater strength of purpose if you go forth knowing "the Lord hath sent me"?

THE LORD STILL SENDS

In the fall of 1995, while talking with a group of pastors in a Brooklyn diner, someone asked about my future plans. I replied,

"God is leading me to start a church in Manhattan." I was excited about the opportunity to reach the nations of the world in New York City's most strategic borough. I just did not know what neighborhood. A man sitting directly across the table exclaimed, "You ought to pray about starting a church in Chelsea!" I had never seen him before that day and have not seen him since, but he grew up in that community and had a burden for it. I had also never heard of the Chelsea area of Manhattan, but the Lord divinely arranged my rendezvous with that man. I asked him questions about Chelsea and jotted down notes. When I began prayerfully surveying the streets, my heart pounded with a sense that God was calling me to start a church there. I soon found a meeting place and Heritage Baptist Church was born in an unassuming second floor YMCA classroom on 23rd Street and 7th Avenue. I have clearly sensed that "the Lord hath sent me" into this community. The challenging years I've spent here have convinced me that the Lord still sends His servants to specific places at appointed times with a biblical message for needy souls who seem to have no interest in what we have to say. It also reminds me of what Elijah must have faced in Bethel and Jericho on the last day of his life (2 Kings 2:23).

YOUR TEETH ARE FALLING OUT OF YOUR HEAD!

While I passed out tracts in Union Square, a well-dressed stranger had stopped to taunt me. "Look at you, your skin is pale," he said earnestly, "your gums look diseased. Your teeth look like they are falling out of your head! If I could have you analyzed by a psychiatrist, I bet they would find you mentally ill!" His diatribe continued: "You are only doing this because your life is such a mess. You must have nothing else to do. You are probably not married and never will be, either."

I told him, "Well, that is not true because I have a beautiful wife, and I can only hope that you love your wife as much as I love mine."

This was not the answer he anticipated, so he fired another question: "Do you have any children?"

"Yes, I have three great kids."

"Then why aren't you at home with them? That is where you should be." Then he asked skeptically, "Are your parents still living?"

"Yes," I said, "I have a very good relationship with them. I love them very much."

His cynicism continued: "Oh, most people who pass out tracts like you don't relate properly with family. I have studied religion and have you all figured out. If I went to your house for one hour, I would find that you are a big hypocrite. So, what are you good at, anyway?"

"I am a preacher of the gospel of Jesus Christ."

He ridiculed me, "I have been listening to you talk, and I don't think you are a very good speaker!" He then continued to launch questions at me: "Do you have any brothers or sisters? What time do you wake up in the morning? Do you get paid out of the offerings your church takes?"

I sought to share Christ with him and ask him some questions, but it was a one-sided interrogation. When my answers did not correspond to his prejudices, he attacked my physical appearance. The last thing he said to me was, "Be sure you take your children to the dentist so that their teeth won't fall out too!"

It was difficult for me to listen to his mockery, and I was glad when he finally moved on. The afternoon proved worthwhile when a couple visited our church the following Sunday after receiving a gospel tract that night! Even more important, when it appears that many scorn the Word of God, I am confident that "the Lord hath sent me" into this community to preach the gospel. Knowing this gives me grace to deal with any petty ridicule I face.

IF THE LORD HAS SENT YOU, GO

How can we be certain of God's will today and live by the motto "The Lord hath sent me"? As God's people, we do not visibly see His cloud by day or His pillar of fire by night like Israel did in their wilderness journey (Numbers 9:15–23). Neither do we audibly hear His voice. But God still has a definite plan for each of His children and a specific place of service for every saint. We have the indwelling Holy Spirit to lead us (Romans 8:14–16, 26–27). We possess the Word of God that can abide richly in us, lighting our way in a dark world (Psalm 119:105). We also have a personal relationship with the Lord Jesus Christ, Who forever lives to intercede for us as our Great High Priest (Hebrews 4:14–16). These truths should lead us to die daily to our desires and live as a sacrifice for Him. God yearns for us to walk in obedience to Him with absolute trust in the Lord Jesus Christ. Live as one crucified with Christ so that you do not conform yourself after the ways of this world (Galatians 2:20; Romans 12:1–2).

An action step every Christian ought to take daily is to surrender himself or herself to God and His will. Isaiah submitted to God, "Here am I; send me," before God sent him anywhere (Isaiah 6:8). Volunteer to do God's will today and then stay there with your eyes on Him. This will ensure that you will live every day right up to your final one going where God has sent you.

How can you determine if the Lord wants you to be a missionary or in the ministry full time? First, seek God's face and pray as Moses: "If I have found grace in thy sight, shew me now thy way" (Exodus 33:13). Involve yourself with people in ministry where you are. Volunteer to serve in as many areas as possible in your local church. Teach Sunday school and children's church; get involved in church outreach with the homeless or evangelistic ministries. Carry tracts with you wherever you go. You will never be a useful servant for God "across the seas" until you are first willing to serve Him "across the street." Humbly receive godly

> You will never be a useful servant for God "across the seas" until you are first willing to serve Him "across the street."

counsel from your spiritual leaders—your parents, your pastor, or a respected Christian example. Survey a field of service that God places on your heart. Take a mission trip with other Christians. Search the Scriptures for a word from God that confirms His will. God does have a place of service for you, and He can confirm that place in your soul by His ever-living and ever-speaking Word. As you "let the peace of God rule in your hearts" and "let the word of Christ dwell in you richly in all wisdom," God's gracious care, real presence, and clear guidance will be demonstrated in your life (Colossians 3:15–16).

What if you feel called to missionary service but don't have a specific geographic call? I have met young people who have surrendered to go to the mission field, but they do not have a distinct sense of where. Many end up going nowhere. I encourage them, "Go somewhere, go anywhere!" Jesus said, "Go." The Great

Commission is not a narrow call but a call to every nation and any culture. Paul went out on his first missionary journey not knowing where he was going. He received a specific geographic call on his second missionary journey only after the Lord forbade his going to Asia and Bithynia (Acts 16:7–9). Adoniram Judson headed to India but arrived in Burma. You also may arrive where you ought to be when you move from where you are not supposed to be. If the Lord has sent you, go and God will crystallize the call along the way. In the meantime, do not forget that it is impossible to bring the gospel to the wrong city.

HUDSON TAYLOR'S MOMENT OF SURRENDER

Hudson Taylor served God with extraordinary fervor by establishing the China Inland Mission, which pierced into the heart of China's multitudes. God used him because he realized that the Lord Jesus Christ had absolute authority over his life. Taylor was seventeen years old when he dedicated himself to God for missionary service. Listen to what he said of his moment of surrender in 1849:

> Well do I remember . . . how in the gladness of my heart I poured out my soul before God, and again and again confessing my grateful love to Him who had done everything for me. . . . I besought Him to give me some work for Him, as an outlet for love and gratitude; some self-denying service, no matter what it might be, *however trying or however trivial*; something with which He would be pleased, and that I might do for Him who had done so much for me. Well do I remember, as in unreserved consecration I put myself, my life, my friends, my all upon the altar, the deep solemnity that came over my soul with the assurance that my offering was accepted. *The presence of*

God became unutterably real and blessed, and I well remember stretching myself on the ground and lying there before Him with unspeakable awe and unspeakable joy. For what service I was accepted I knew not. *But a deep consciousness that I was not my own took possession of me, which has never since been effaced*[1] (emphasis mine).

Taylor attached no strings to his surrender to God. When God's presence becomes "unutterably real," we too will have "unspeakable joy," and we will know we are not our own. When we know this fact, we will follow Him and go where He sends us, regardless of how trivial or trial-filled our service may be. Do not think that God sends only special people like Elijah or Hudson Taylor to do certain tasks. God has a purpose for you. "For we are His workmanship, created in Christ Jesus unto good works, which God hath before ordained that we should walk in them" (Ephesians 2:10). One of the great joys in life is to confidently know that "the Lord hath sent me" and that you have obeyed His call. As a result you are in the heart of God's will, seeing Him at work and functioning as His servant, standing on eternity's edge.

REFLECTIONS FOR TODAY

Obediently follow God because "the Lord sends" is fundamental to living on eternity's edge. Make sure that you are surrendered to the will of God in unreserved consecration without any strings attached. Be willing to do anything God wants, however trying or trivial, for He has done so much for you.

MEMORIZE

Isaiah 6:8 "Also I heard the voice of the Lord, saying, Whom shall I send, and who will go for us? Then said I, Here am I; send me."

MEDITATE

Meditate on the following Scripture verses.

1. According to Romans 8:14–16, in what way does the Holy Spirit lead you?

2. According to Galatians 2:20, in what way are you crucified with Christ and how does Christ living in you change you on the inside?

3. According to Colossians 3:15–17, how are we to allow Christ's word to dwell richly in us and what changes occur when we delight ourselves in His Word?

Dear heavenly Father,
Grant me Your grace to follow Your direction in spite of the many forces in this world that are against Your plan. Thank You, Lord Jesus, for Your great love to lay down Your life for me through Your death on the cross. I praise You for Your power to raise Yourself up from the dead. Teach me today to be crucified with You so that Your Word may abide richly in my life. Direct me in a clear path so that I may bring forth much fruit and glorify Your name. In Jesus' name, Amen.

6 Discipling the Next Generation . . . On Eternity's Edge

"The sons of the prophets . . ." (2 Kings 2:3, 5, 15)

David Hosaflook slept in my home one night in the early 1990s, and I am glad he did. I lived five minutes from Kennedy Airport, and since he was flying out from there, my home was a convenient stop. David was going as a pioneer missionary to Albania, a spiritually and materially impoverished nation. Once he arrived on the field, I received his prayer letters, and over the years, I have admired him in his faithful evangelism and discipleship of Albanians, who live in difficult circumstances. Some of these believers now shepherd churches in the mountainous regions of Albania. David defines discipleship as "time spent with a new Christian helping him to become a Christian; a show-and-tell relationship in which one Christian exemplifies and explains new life to another." He calls his institute "Hodgepodge Bible Institute" because of the variety of sources and methods he uses. To David, discipleship is not just a program but a lifestyle investment into others' lives. It is his heart ministering to the hearts of those around him, his life being poured into and reproduced in the precious souls of Albanians.

ELIJAH'S VISION

During the days of the judges, Samuel established schools for young prophets, but the enrollment apparently declined during the dark days of Israel's idolatry.[1] After Samuel, nearly two hundred years passed and the schools faded into near extinction. Dust and cobwebs filled the empty dwellings until Elijah woke up the schools with his visionary heart. When God promised Elijah on Mount Horeb that seven thousand still had not bowed their knee to Baal, the rejuvenated prophet reinstituted the schools and worked for their increase right through his final earthly hours. These schools attracted spiritually hungry young prophets bursting with potential, and the discipling of these men revealed the heart of Elijah. He poured himself into preparing these young men for ministry. These prophetic schools became God's "still small voice" to the nation; that is, they did not appear outwardly spectacular like a "strong wind," "an earthquake," or "a fire" that Elijah had experienced on Mount Sinai nor were they the result of any miracle, but they were quietly effective in bringing God's Word to a land in spiritual famine (1 Kings 19:11–18). These dedicated preachers gathered to study God's law and then scattered to proclaim it to the nation.[2] On his last earthly day, Elijah flung himself one last time into the gap of opportunity, filling these young men with hope, defending the faith, and teaching them to contend for it as well.

Interestingly, Elisha and the sons of the prophets knew that Elijah would depart. Like someone who has heard news that he thinks others do not know, the sons of the prophets made a mad dash to Elisha in the cities of Bethel and Jericho to say, "Knowest thou that the Lord will take away thy master from thy head today?" (2 Kings 2:3, 5). We do not know how they knew this, but God often communicated directly to prophets and

He may have told them. Although losing Elijah from among them would create a huge void, one can imagine that his departure created incredible excitement for them in their continuing ministry. Elijah's transport into heaven by a whirlwind would encourage them in the difficult days ahead, instilling a lively hope for heaven in their hearts. It would also stabilize them to face future threats, enlivening them to a fresh sense of purpose to confront life's brevity with passion.

These schools revealed the vision of Elijah. They demonstrated his concern not to build an empire to impress others with his greatness but to build up individuals to see God's greatness during his life and after he was gone. Beware of the person who is not concerned for the condition of the people or ministry that follows him. The leader who lives self-centeredly, caring only for his reputation and comfort, lives fatally. Elijah's burden centered upon the next generation, the hope of Israel's future. Some of his students were impressionable and needed to see strength. Some were arrogant and needed to see humility. Elijah's focus was on those who would follow him in the schools. He did not want them to die out as they had after Samuel; he longed for their continuance. Elijah's dream was realized, for after his transfer to heaven, the schools of the prophets continued to expand in influence.[3]

> **The leader who lives self-centeredly, caring only for his reputation and comfort, lives fatally.**

ELIJAH THE HEART-TURNER

In the book of Malachi, the last book written by a Jewish prophet, Malachi completes the Hebrew Scripture with an amazing prophecy of God sending forth Elijah before the second coming of the Messiah: "Behold, I will send you Elijah the prophet before the coming of the great and dreadful day of the Lord: and he shall turn the heart of the fathers to the children, and the heart of the children to their fathers, lest I come and smite the earth with a curse" (Malachi 4:5–6).

Because this will be Elijah's ministry before the day of the Lord, we can conclude that it was also his ministry as he moved from city to city on the last day of his life. In fact, these students were known as "the sons of the prophets" (2 Kings 2:3, 5, 7, 15). Elijah was a heart-turner. His message turned the heart of the fathers to their children so that the children turned their hearts to their fathers and even more importantly, to their fathers' God.

We can only imagine what this turner of hearts said to these sons of the prophets in Gilgal, Jericho, and Bethel on his last day. Maybe some were discouraged because of the increasing number of enemies in the land who said that "there is no help . . . in God" (Psalm 3:2). With a compassionate yet firm voice, Elijah could answer this faith-staggering suggestion with God's Word and his own life experience. Confidently, he would have pointed them to David's God, Who said they need not fear ten thousand who were against them: God is "a shield for me; my glory, and the lifter up of mine head" (Psalm 3:3). Or maybe there was a young prophet newly married with financial problems. Another was single, struggling with loneliness. I can imagine one who started out on fire for God, but in his busyness to do the work of the Lord, he had forgotten the Lord of the work. Apathy had set in. I can envision another young prophet disillusioned that there seemed to be more mockers than believers among the younger generation. With a tired voice, he might have said to Elijah, "The work is small and goes so slow, what use is it? I am bored with trying." Elijah may well have answered, "Wait on the Lord: be of good courage, and he shall strengthen thine heart. Draw near to God, young men, God is a mighty warrior, and you have what it takes to fulfill the spiritual battles before you." I can almost hear Elijah say, "Blessed are they that keep his testimonies, and that seek him with the whole heart" (Psalm 119:2). And so it went. Elijah heard from their hearts, and he answered from his, right up to his last day, pouring himself and his precious final moments of earthly time into the future of his beloved land.

DISCIPLESHIP CONCERNS YOU

We likewise are called to both be and make disciples. This concerns every Christian because it is the crux of the Great Commission: "Go ye therefore, and teach all nations, baptizing them in the name of the Father, and of the Son, and of the Holy Ghost: teaching them to observe all things whatsoever I have commanded you: and, lo, I am with you alway, even unto the end of the world. Amen" (Matthew 28:19–20). There is one main verb in the Great Commission: *teach*. This is an active imperative, or a direct command, which means that everyone who follows Christ should personally contribute to this exciting opportunity. *Go*, *baptizing*, and *teaching* are participles that modify *teach*. In other words, going, baptizing, and instructing are essential to making disciples.

The Greek word *mathete*—commonly translated "disciple" in the New Testament—refers to one who learns, "indicating thought accompanied by endeavor. A disciple was not only a pupil, but an adherent; hence they are spoken of as imitators of their teacher (John 8:31; 15:8)."[4] A Christian disciple is a believer in the Lord Jesus Christ who hungers to grow in conformity to Him, seeks to evangelize others, and works to conserve the fruit of his labor. There is a high cost of discipleship, for Jesus taught that we cannot be His disciple unless we love Him with an unrivaled love, daily bear our cross, and willingly forsake all that we have for His sake (Luke 14:25–33).

A disciple should be engaged in "discipleship," which is the process of helping others grow into spiritual maturity with accountability by fellowshiping with God and with others. "*Mathetes* always implies the existence of a personal attachment"; discipleship is not possible without building and growing relationships with other individuals and the Lord.[5] Paul expressed the heartbeat of a disciple-maker when he wrote to the Galatian believers, "My little children, of whom I travail in birth again until Christ be formed in you" (Galatians 4:19). Elijah also was driven by this happy, divine anguish on his last day, desiring for the sons of the prophets and those in apostate Israel to have more of God's power and presence manifest in them.

DISCIPLING YOUNG BELIEVERS

Florio didn't have a church home. He had become a believer in Jesus Christ while in his homeland of Haiti, but he failed to grow spiritually. He relocated to New York and continued drifting from his Savior while living in a tough drug-infested city project and studying architecture at City College in Manhattan. Like so many Christians, Florio's goals were more important than God's purposes. I met him while evangelizing in his Queens neighborhood and invited him to the church I pastored at the time, just two blocks from his apartment. Realizing he had gone his own way long enough, he came to Parkway

Baptist Church. Quickly he grew in faith, showing a thirst to know Christ and live God's Word.

When Florio suddenly disappeared from our services, I tracked him down and found that a college campus cult had nearly turned him aside from God's grace. They taught him that baptism was necessary for salvation, and he had followed their teaching and was on the verge of leaving our church. I began discipling Florio and realized that I had not made the necessary ministry investment in his spiritual maturity. He soon became active again in serving the Lord, and one afternoon we went to the hospital to pray with one of our members who was dying of cancer. That visit placed a deep burden for service to Christ in Florio's heart. Driving home from Manhattan, he announced, "I believe God wants me in ministry for Him. I see what is truly important. People need salvation and the only hope for a dying man is Jesus Christ and His Word." As Levi Matthew left his tax collecting business upon hearing Christ's command, "Follow me," Florio forsook his architecture studies and began preparing for the gospel ministry.

After graduating, he joined the United States army to serve as a chaplain and was deployed to the Persian Gulf region in our conflict to remove Saddam Hussein from power. Florio marched into Baghdad with the main infantry unit and was there the day the statue of Saddam Hussein was pulled down before a watching world. The Lord has opened many doors for Florio to preach Christ to our soldiers. Recently he wrote to me the following exciting report:

> We have seen the faithfulness of God in our midst. Last week a Senior Non-Commissioned Officer kneeled with me in my office and sincerely begged Christ to save him.

He is prospering in the faith through discipleship. Our Base Commander led an Army Specialist to the Lord yesterday. In a praise meeting that we had in Church last week, four Soldiers trusted Christ as their personal Savior. These are just a few of the many miracles and answers to prayer that we see on a weekly basis here in Iraq. I believe these godly men are dedicated and they know the battle belongs to the Lord, and this is why they make this a priority to meet and pray in the morning.[6]

ELIJAH'S VISION STILL BEARS FRUIT

Elijah's school of the prophets planted in the heart of cities diseased with idolatry has been a model for theological schools, seminaries, Sunday schools, and many other kinds of institutes for thousands of years. His schools were not huge; Jericho's school had an enrollment of fifty men, a small number compared to the mega-church ministries all around us. His vision has born fruit for uncounted millions of souls up to the present. The Lord led me to start a church-based ministry we call the Heritage Discipleship Institute. My purpose is to disciple those who are members of Christ and who aspire to do ministry for Him. It is a small and slow work, but it satisfies my soul to pour myself into those who now serve Christ as deacons, adult Bible teachers, children's ministry leaders, faithful witnesses, and mothers or fathers. This institute identifies those with a servant's heart, encourages local church ministry, grounds young believers in their faith, and influences our people to study God's Word more intensely. It has been God's still small voice in our local church.

Dameon heard me on our Heritage of Faith radio broadcast and attended our Heritage Discipleship Institute. Soon he began attending our church, and he now serves as a deacon and fervent soulwinner. Hilary started attending our church and, soon after, our institute. She now leads a dynamic women's adult Bible fellowship class and disciples other women in a Friday night Bible study. Edgar came and now serves as a deacon and Spanish adult Bible fellowship teacher. Jorge recently began coming, and he zealously invites many of his friends to Heritage. Helen graduated and is solidly grounded, serving the Lord in many capacities in our church.

DISCIPLING OUR CHILDREN

In our day we desperately need a generation of men and women who will actively turn their hearts to their children. I have found that being a parent is an exhausting and difficult work. Many times we fail, but discipling the next generation begins in the home. When parents are neglectful, abusive, or overly permissive, they will provoke their children to wrath (Ephesians 6:4). Children turn their backs on their parents most often when parents first turn their time and attention away from their children. Parents, do you take an interest in training your children in God's Word? Do you have family prayer? Do you memorize Scripture in your home? Do you sing songs? Do you play games or read books? As we bring up our children in the nurture (loving discipline) and admonition (loving instruction) of the Lord, they will be inclined to become saved and serve Him. "We will not hide them from their children, showing to the generation to come the praises of the Lord, and his strength, and his wonderful works that he hath done" (Psalm 78:4).

Parents are the key to discipling the next generation. In no way do I minimize the

> **Parents are the key to discipling the next generation.**

role of the mother as a guide for her home, but the father must be the leader and main disciple-maker of his children. For good or bad, whether he speaks one word or many, a father will teach his children many things. Oh, that fathers who know Christ personally will seek to make Him known to their children! Fathers are needed to be active and not passive; they must love and not abuse; they must be content and not adulterous. Do you remember Hiel? He was the Bethelite father who buried his sons in Jericho's foundations to appease Baal (1 Kings 16:34). His shameful murder exemplifies to us the selfishness and abuse that idolatry brings. Similarly, a father who commits adultery abandons and wounds his entire family. Fathers who pursue their pleasure and seek material gain ultimately abandon their children much like Hiel did, even though they don't kill them physically. Fathers are needed who will live and love Christ and communicate to their sons, "You have what it takes to be the man God wants." Every son must hear from his father that he can live for Christ and be a success for God in a hostile world. Fathers must delight in their daughters and assure them in word and deed that they are beautiful in God's sight. Every daughter wants to feel treasured and wanted by her parents but especially by her dad.[7] Providing a loving home where Christ is known will go a long way to discipling our children so that they serve their own "generation by the will of God" (Acts 13:36). Parents, are you living holy for God? Are you confident God can raise up your children to serve Christ?

Philip Henry went through the entire Bible, teaching it chapter by chapter to his children, accompanying it with prayer and singing. The sound of singing, he said, was a distinct confession that a family loved to praise the Lord. This teaching was difficult work, but it paid off. Matthew, Philip's son, wrote a famous commentary based on the notes taken from his father's teaching. Matthew Henry said, "They who pray in the family, do well; they who read and pray, do better; but they who sing, and read, and pray, do best of all."[8]

Do not excuse yourself from making disciples, either among new believers or your children. As you follow Christ, find others with this passion and then pour yourself into them. Elijah was not discouraged from seeking those who would not bow to the idols of his day. Today there are many around us who yearn to be Christlike. Be open-minded about using your valuable time with others. Believe in the importance of discipleship and desire to be used in helping others grow into the image of Christ. Discipleship begins the moment of your salvation and will continue until either Jesus returns or you die. This is central to the Great Commission and the heartbeat of the local church. It is incumbent upon everyone who follows Christ. This command is not for religious professionals or pastors only but for everyone who believes that "all power . . . in heaven and earth" is given to the risen Lord Jesus Christ (Matthew 28:18).

REFLECTIONS FOR TODAY

Discipling the next generation is vital for living on eternity's edge. Make time for family devotions where you can sing, read Scripture, and pray with your family. Begin discipling your sons and daughters living in your own home.

MEMORIZE

Psalm 78:6–7 "That the generation to come might know them, even the children which should be born; who should arise and declare them to their children: that they might set their hope in God, and not forget the works of God, but keep his commandments."

MEDITATE

Meditate on Psalm 78:1–8. This passage is a great challenge for parents to pass on the testimony of God's Word to their children.

1. In Psalm 78:4–5, what are parents to show to their children and why?

2. In verses 6–7, what should be the goal of teaching God's Word to our children?

Lord of the harvest,
Give me the power of Your Holy Spirit that I may fulfill
the Great Commission by going and making disciples for
You. May I begin in my own home, and may You give
me compassion to reach out to every creature who needs
You. You must give me the strength and wisdom because
I do not have what it takes to accomplish this task. But I
know that through You and with You I can do all things
because You strengthen me. In Jesus' name, Amen.

7 Training Leaders . . . On Eternity's Edge

"I will not leave thee. . . . They still went on, and talked" (2 Kings 2:2*b*, 11*b*)

Bryan and I launched out together and preached on the city subways. We would enter a subway car and give a brief message whizzing along in the underground tunnel. We moved from car to car until we had preached in all of them, distributing gospel tracts and offering free New Testaments; then we would hop on another train and do it all over again. This adventure, during my ministry at City View Baptist Church in Brooklyn, stirred our hearts for the people in our city. Bryan was already a mature Christian, but ministering on the subways gave him the sweet taste of publicly proclaiming God's powerful gospel. After I left City View, Bryan continued in the ministry of the Word; when the next pastor left, Bryan took leadership of the church and now serves as their shepherd. Watching Bryan grow taught me that God wants me involved in other people's lives so that I can help them become what He wants them to be. We may be mentoring future leaders and not even be aware of it!

A TENACITY TEST

On his last day Elijah made three similar yet challenging statements to mentor Elisha. The first is found in 2 Kings 2:2: "And Elijah said unto Elisha, *Tarry here*, I pray thee; for the Lord hath sent me to Bethel." He says the same thing before going to Jericho and Jordan. "*Tarry here*, I pray thee; for the Lord hath sent me to Bethel . . . to Jericho . . . to Jordan" (verses 4, 6; emphasis mine). What was the purpose of Elijah's puzzling petition in asking Elisha to stay behind? One may think that Elijah was motivated by humility and that Elijah simply "wished to experience this honor alone."[1] But we see that Elijah was giving his disciple one final test before Elisha could replace him. Elisha had to see Elijah depart (verse 10). The issue before Elisha on that day was unmistakable: was he qualified to be Elijah's successor? Elisha had to remain with Elijah throughout his final day to see his leader taken up into heaven and consequently for him to inherit Elijah's ministry. Elijah's request was a tenacity test to measure Elisha's desire for service.

When Elijah first met Elisha, the young man promised, "I will follow thee" (1 Kings 19:20); then "he arose, and went after Elijah, and ministered unto him" (1 Kings 19:21). Elijah tested Elisha's grit: would he walk in God's will? Did he possess a divided heart? Was he controlled by God's Spirit? Would he follow his mentor faithfully to the end? In order to stand against the convenience of Jeroboam's counterfeit faith, Elisha would need to endure hardness and overcome man's natural tendency toward "flowery beds of ease."[2] To refuse the seduction of popularity found in Baal worship, he would require a heart to do the right thing when confronted with self-will options.

SHOULDER TO SHOULDER

Elijah was not the only one who knew he was living his last day. His apprentice Elisha knew it, too, and so did all the "sons of the prophets" in Bethel and in Jericho (2 Kings 2:3, 5). Elijah escorted his closest disciple on a ministry tour, showing him step by step how to live boldly for God, guiding Elisha to the training centers for young prophets established in the cities of Gilgal, Bethel, and Jericho. Finally, he would show Elisha how to leave this world. Everything that happened on that last day developed in Elisha a thirst for ministry and a hunger for a personal relationship with God. Elisha learned from his teacher both how to run the race and how to finish it.

Elisha responded three times to Elijah's test with great conviction: "As the Lord liveth, and as thy soul liveth, I will not leave thee" (2 Kings 2:2, 4, 6). Elisha did not want to miss the once-in-a-lifetime opportunity to be with Elijah on his last day. These men loved one another as a father loves his son or as a brother loves brother. Elisha did not presume to know better than Elijah by responding, "You are going to Bethel? I don't see the sense of that, so I will stay behind. That city is full of young men who scorn the God we believe. I won't waste my time going there" (2 Kings 2:23). Or when Elijah announced his intention to go to Jericho, Elisha refuses to chide him sarcastically: "Jericho? But the water there is undrinkable and the ground is unfruitful. We will go thirsty and hungry there, so I will stay here" (2 Kings 2:19). Elisha's commitment, reflected in the words "I will not leave thee," shows "tenacity of purpose" to stay beside Elijah.[3] It would have been easier for Elijah to move Mount Carmel into the Mediterranean Sea than to get Elisha to leave him. In 2 Kings 2:1 we read that "Elijah went with Elisha from Gilgal." They walked shoulder to shoulder throughout this final day, just as they had done many days before, since Elisha had sacrificed his earthly livelihood to follow God.

A DISCIPLESHIP SECRET

Elijah provides for us a practical secret in the discipling of new leaders. Discipleship is not an event but a process of taking the time to pour your life into another. The learner must listen and labor alongside the mentor. Until the moment Elijah ascended in the chariot, he and Elisha "went on, and talked" (2 Kings 2:11). Training did not take place only in the structured confines of a classroom but on the dusty roads between the cities of Bethel and Jericho. Or on the dry ground of the Jordan River, or on the road east of the Jordan. I imagine they had a lot to discuss and many praises to offer God after they walked through and then beyond the Jordan River together! Similarly, training leaders can take place as we live our daily lives: in a restaurant during lunch, walking along a city sidewalk, traveling in the subway, or meeting informally in our home or office.

I often struggle with exactly how to go about training others for ministry. Honestly, I cannot even say that I have done it very successfully. Elijah can encourage us because he lived out something very simple. Be present. Give time to faithful men who will be able to teach others also. With only one day to live, Elijah did not go covert and hide. He did not focus on what would be and overlook the opportunity in what was. He redeemed the time "because the days are evil" (Ephesians 5:16). Time is a limited commodity that can be invested or squandered, and the present moment is the only time we have. C. S. Lewis wrote that "the Present is the point at which time touches eternity . . . for the Past is frozen and no longer flows, and the Present is all lit up with eternal rays."[4] Live in the present every day. Do not dwell on past regrets, failures, and sins. Knowing no tomorrow, Elijah was out in the open and transparent, walking side by side with Elisha. He looked him in the eye and spoke faith-building words. We too can speak up. Three times "Elijah said unto Elisha" (2 Kings 2:2, 4, 6). Take the initiative. I ask myself if I tenderly seek out quiet moments to speak to my wife and lead her spiritually before the presence of God? Lovingly, have I sought out quiet moments to listen to my teenage children to see what is on their hearts? Prayerfully, have I taken the initiative to spend time with those who lead ministries or have questions in our church? When was the last time you asked someone, "Ask what I shall do for thee?" By speaking up, Elijah made himself available to assist others in their daily battles.

Four Steps in Jesus' Training of the Twelve

Consider the model that Jesus Christ left us in reproducing Himself in the lives of the twelve apostles. He used four distinct steps in His training of these disciples. First, there was the "come and see" step. In John 1:35–51, six of Jesus' future apostles meet Him for the first time: John and Andrew, James and Peter, and Philip and Bartholomew. When John and Andrew inquired where Jesus dwelt, the Lord answered, "Come and see." Here, the young disciples gained information, listened, and initially believed on the Lord Jesus Christ. We can only imagine what it would have been like to spend an entire day with Jesus, sitting at His feet and soaking in His words. This initial phase took the entire first year of Jesus' earthly ministry.

The next step of leadership is "come and follow me." After spending one year with the Lord, the disciples demonstrated a greater level of commitment to serve alongside Him. Mark 1:17–18 records Jesus' words to His disciples, "Come ye after me, and I will make you to become fishers of men. . . . They forsook their nets, and followed him." At this level there was self-denial of secular pursuits. Jesus showed them how to fish, and they involved themselves with Jesus as learners.

At the half-way point of Jesus' earthly ministry, He called the Twelve to be His apostles. This third step is "come and be with me." "And he ordained twelve, that they should be with him, and that he might send them forth to preach" (Mark 3:14). The calling of the Twelve was a landmark moment in the earthly ministry of Jesus Christ. "It divides the ministry of our Lord into two portions, nearly equal, probably, as to duration, but unequal as to the extent and importance of the work done in each respectively."[5] Once Jesus called His "apostles," they went forth as sheep into the midst of a wolf pack (Matthew 10:16). Jesus took a divine risk in giving His followers power against unclean spirits, sickness, and disease as He told them to be wise as serpents and harmless as doves (Matthew 10:1, 16). They identified themselves as Christ's and labored for Him. The final step in their training was this: "Remain in me and go into the world to make disciples." They were independent from the physical presence of Christ and dependent upon the Holy Spirit's power. They were leaders, ready to make disciples of all the nations and ethnic groups of the world (Matthew 28:19–20). Even this took the Lord of glory three and a half years of intense training, teaching, and time to accomplish.[6] In studying Christ's ministry, we discover that Elijah's ministry is Christlike: neither wanted mere followers but discipled faithful men who would be listeners, gaining information, learners by being involved, laborers identified with the prophet, and finally leaders, independent from his physical presence but able to teach others also.

A Man Like Moses

As God opened up the Red Sea when Moses lifted up "the rod of God," so God used Elijah to split the Jordan River with his prophet's cloak. Both men saw the Lord miraculously provide food. Moses ate manna; Elijah survived drought, fed of ravens and widows. Each bore the heavy pressure of leadership, and under that weight, they both asked to die: Moses prayed, "Kill me, I pray thee" (Numbers 11:15), and similarly, Elijah prayed, "It is enough; now, O Lord, take away my life" (1 Kings 19:4). Both were closely related to the law. Moses received the law from God, and Elijah called the Israelites to return to the law. Each had unusual departures from earth. "As God Himself buried Moses, and his grave has not been found to this day, so does He fetch Elijah to heaven in a still more glorious manner in a fiery chariot with fiery horses, so that fifty men, who searched for him, did not find him on the earth."[7] Finally, Elijah and Moses miraculously appeared together on the Mount of Transfiguration and spoke of Jesus' salvation work (Luke 9:28–30). Elijah was clearly a man like Moses.

Perhaps their most significant similarity is that they both prepared another individual to lead the people of God farther than they had. Just as Moses brilliantly instructed Joshua to lead the next generation out of the wilderness and into the Land of Promise, Elijah trained Elisha to carry on the work of bringing God's law to an apostate Israel. At the heart of Moses' training was time spent with Joshua. Joshua spent so much time with Moses that he was called "Moses' minister" (Joshua 1:1), which is the same word used to describe Elisha's service toward Elijah (1 Kings 19:21). Joshua spent time with Moses in prayer as Moses talked with God face to face (Exodus 33:11). Moses spent forty years with Joshua, proving him in the furnace of the wilderness, verifying his faithfulness and fortitude to God. When God buried His worker Moses, His work flourished because Joshua was clearly the next God-called leader for the wandering nation of Israel. This ability to give the eternal Word of God to the next generation separates a good leader from a great one.

Passing on God's eternal purpose is a most complex aspect of leadership. It is no coincidence that of all men, it was Elijah who appeared with Moses and Jesus on that mount. There stood two of the greatest leaders this world has ever known along with the only begotten Son of God. Pray daily for God to give you a Joshua, an Elisha, or a Peter to mentor so that God's Word will faithfully be proclaimed to subsequent generations. Or maybe you are an Elisha who needs to find an Elijah to disciple you. Pray for God to lead you to someone who can be an example of faithfulness.

> **Passing on God's eternal purpose is a most complex aspect of leadership.**

SOMEBODY NEEDS YOU

Elijah's last day challenges us to get caught up in the needs of other people. Throughout Scripture we see the ministry of mentoring. Barnabas mentored Paul. Paul mentored Timothy and countless others. Jesus mentored the Twelve and they turned the world upside down. On the last day of his life, Elijah completed his mentoring of Elisha. "Iron sharpeneth iron; so a man sharpeneth the countenance of his friend" (Proverbs 27:17). Remember this: somebody needs you to lift him or her up. People are ready to serve the Lord if we will find them and establish them in eternal truth. This relationship between

Elijah and Elisha was ideal for both men; Elijah gained physical assistance and Elisha gained spiritual insight. The older generation needs the energy of youth; the younger generation needs the maturity of experience. Elijah did not stop spending time with Elisha, leading, speaking and preparing him to step into his place. And Elisha did not stop following his leader. Living on eternity's edge, Elijah labored side by side with Elisha so that eternal truth would be remembered, preserved, and propagated to the nations of the earth.

REFLECTIONS FOR TODAY

Preparing leaders to follow in our steps is a key for living on eternity's edge. Make time to listen to God's speaking through His Word. Share what you read from Scripture with someone else today.

MEMORIZE

2 Timothy 2:2 "And the things that thou hast heard of me among many witnesses, the same commit thou to faithful men, who shall be able to teach others also."

MEDITATE

Meditate on 2 Timothy 2. This letter is Paul's epistle written on his edge of eternity. In giving his final instructions of discipleship to Timothy, Paul gave seven pictures of a Christian. Beside each Christian portrait, think about a blessing or a challenge to you in your walk with the Lord today. The first one is filled in to assist you in this meditation.

1. A strong son? *2 Timothy 2:1–2: The blessing is to have the honor of committing God's Word to faithful men. I am challenged to examine my life with this question: Am I teaching others and making disciples through my life and example today?*

2. A dedicated soldier (vv. 3–4)?

3. A victorious athlete (v. 5)?

4. A laboring farmer (vv. 6–10)?

5. A diligent student (vv. 15–19)?

6. A valuable vessel (vv. 20–22)?

7. A gentle servant (vv. 23–25)?

God of eternity,
Help me to have a resolute heart to stay beside You, my Savior and Lord of all! Teach me to vigilantly train others in my daily life. Give me a Joshua or an Elisha to build up in the faith. Fill me with Your Spirit that my life will be a living reminder of our Lord Jesus Christ. Today, may I live on eternity's edge, focused on what is of eternal importance. In Jesus' name, Amen.

8 Living with Assurance . . . On Eternity's Edge

*"Ask what I shall do . . . before I be taken
away from thee"* (2 Kings 2:9*b*)

Although physically blind, Regina's eyes were wide open to see the real world, serving God and others until the day she went home to heaven. Many trials were crammed into her brief life—her two-year-old daughter had died, and one son had hearing and vision problems. But she never complained, and as a blind woman she excelled in the business world and in raising her three sons for Jesus. She never protested God's providential dealings, even when she contracted terminal cancer. On what turned out to be the last day of her life, she told her husband, Thomas, "The doctor said I can go home today." When Thomas checked with the doctor, he was told that Regina did not have permission to go home to her Manhattan apartment. Thomas knew that she spoke of heaven. Later that afternoon, one of our faithful members, Josephine, went to pray with Regina. Filled with bodily pain, she still prayed with her heart full of praise, "Lord, thank You for Your goodness!" Because Regina depended upon the finished work of Jesus Christ, she had complete assurance of her salvation and could in everything give thanks. Just as she had told her husband, Regina went home later that day by the goodness of God in Jesus Christ.

Elijah also had unwavering confidence that he was going to heaven. Second Kings 2:1 begins, "And it came to pass, when the Lord would take up Elijah into heaven by a whirlwind." A whirlwind speaks of God's personal revealing of Himself.[1] When we learn that a hurricane is moving towards us, we naturally steer clear of its path. Elijah had no need to run from this perfect storm, for God would use it to usher him into eternal safety.

No Fear

Standing at heaven's brink, the man of God performed his duty without a trace of terror. Divine peace permeated his being; he worked as if he had ten years of ministry remaining, not just a few hours. Make no mistake about it: these verses unambiguously reveal Elijah's keen awareness that his last day was upon him. His last two recorded statements in Scripture relate to his being taken from Elisha. "Ask what I shall do for thee, before I be taken away from thee." Then, "Thou hast asked a hard thing: nevertheless, if thou see me when I am taken from thee, it shall be so unto thee; but if not, it shall not be so" (2 Kings 2:9–10). It is also apparent that Elisha and the sons of the prophets knew that Elijah was living his last day. Twice the younger men asked Elisha, "Knowest thou that the Lord will take away thy master from thy head to day? And he said, Yea, I know it; hold ye your peace" (2 Kings 2:3, 5). One reason that Elisha was at peace is that Elijah had no fear.

Elijah's assurance exemplifies that as believers we will enter heaven at the exact moment God ordains. Are you sure like

Elijah or Regina that your home is heaven? Although Elijah's precise experience is unrepeated in all of human history, his sovereign ascent in a whirlwind models reality for all of God's redeemed. In going directly to heaven Elijah "gave a type and figure of the ascension of Christ

> # Death is our divine appointment with God.

and the opening of the kingdom of heaven to all believers."[2] Elijah shows us that death is a departure, a translation, a crossing. For the believer, death is not an end, but a door, a bridge, a tunnel that leads to the light and glory of heaven. We pass from earth, where we see darkly and know partially, to heaven, where we will see Christ face to face and know fully (1 Corinthians 13:12). For all those born again of the Holy Spirit, to be absent from the body is to be present with the Lord (2 Corinthians 5:8). God providentially decides that moment, for death is our divine appointment with Him: "And as it is appointed unto men once to die, but after this the judgment" (Hebrews 9:27).

Elijah's rapture also foretells the resurrection of the body. This is a purely biblical and Christian doctrine. We surely believe in the immortality of the soul but so do other religions and ancient traditions. Various religions view the soul as living on after the death of the body, either in a heavenly place or floating around overlooking life on earth. Immortality of the soul is not resurrection, and only Christianity teaches the resurrection of the body! Jesus taught that we should not be shocked by this: "Marvel not at this: for the hour is coming, in the which all that are in the graves shall hear his voice, and shall come forth; they that have done good, unto the resurrection of life; and they that have done evil, unto the resurrection of damnation" (John 5:28–29). In God's good time, every body will be raised again and will be brought to heaven or sent to hell to suffer for ever and ever.[3] Believers today await the any-moment appearing of Jesus Christ, when "the Lord himself shall descend from heaven with a shout . . . and the dead in Christ shall rise first: then we which are alive and remain shall be caught up together with them in the clouds, to meet the Lord in the air: so shall we ever be with the Lord" (1 Thessalonians 4:16–17). Our ultimate hope for this is founded on the fact that the resurrection of Jesus was bodily and not merely spiritual. Jesus said after rising from death, "Handle me, and see; for a spirit hath not flesh and bones, as ye see me have" (Luke 24:39). Just as Elijah was bodily caught up in a whirlwind to heaven, so all believers will arise from this world to be caught up with Christ forever. When Jesus returns, our corruptible bodies will be changed into a glorious resurrection body, "according to the working whereby he is able to subdue all things unto himself" (Philippians 3:21). All dust will be subject to His divine will and the bodies of those redeemed by Christ's blood will be remade to live forever with Him in heaven!

HEAVEN, A DAZZLING KINGDOM OF GOD'S GLORY

Elijah's miraculous translation from earth to heaven would have a great impact upon the land of Israel. Just as now, many mockers in Elijah's day doubted an afterlife.[4] His translation testified to the indisputable truth that there is a world beyond that which we can see. Heaven is a real place, a dazzling kingdom of crystal-clear color lit by the glory of our triune God. When our bodies die and sink into the dust, if our spirit is renewed by God, we will rise out of this world into His presence. The redeemed "shall see his face" and we will forever be with Him! (Revelation 22:4). The spirit does not share the grave with the body; our Savior Jesus Christ "hath abolished death, and hath brought life and immortality to light through the gospel" (2 Timothy 1:9–10). If the Lord tarries His coming, we all must face this last enemy of death, and we can be assured that victory over this foe is possible "through our Lord Jesus Christ," Who raised Himself from death (1 Corinthians 15:26, 57). At death, we can also be thankful that there is no limbo, soul sleep, purgatory, or unconsciousness of the soul. Death leads the believer to real and full life "with Christ; which is far better" than anything this life can ever offer (Philippians 1:23).

ARE YOU SURE OF HEAVEN?

Elijah knew he was in the Lord's loving hand, and so can you; for he was a man of like passions as we are. Are you born again through repentance of sin and faith in the perfect righteousness and finished work of the Lord Jesus Christ? Are you sure? When the Holy Spirit dwells in a person by the power of the new birth, then "the Spirit itself beareth witness with our spirit, that we are the children of God" (Romans 8:16). As God teaches us to believe on the name of the Son of God, we may "know" that we have eternal life (1 John 5:13). Jesus said, "My sheep hear my voice, and I know them, and they follow me. And I give unto them eternal life; and they shall never perish, neither shall any man pluck them out of my hand" (John 10:27–28). This assurance is vital. Every child wants to know his family. Every soldier must know for which side he wars. Every athlete knows for what team he competes. Every Christian ought to be assured that God is his Savior from sin if he is to live well on eternity's edge.

You Have a Reason for Being

Elijah's fearless heart helped him maintain his focus right up to his last day. When you have this assurance, you also can live as an overcomer with purpose. Is your life filled with seemingly menial tasks? Do you have a terminal illness? Are you homebound? Are you young but unsure of yourself as you face your future? Are you saddled with debt? Maybe you feel trapped in an office, in a marriage, or in an abusive family. Perhaps you are swamped with changing diapers, doing laundry, and preparing meals. While you were growing up, your father called you "a stupid failure." Should you feel useless? Should you be overcome with the fear of failure or rejection? Absolutely not! Live as the apostle Paul, who said, "In nothing I shall be ashamed, but that with all boldness, as always, so now also Christ shall be magnified in my body, whether it be by life, or by death. For to me to live is Christ, and to die is gain" (Philippians 1:20–21). You can draw near to God in a real and satisfying relationship and pray. You can call others to tell them to follow the Lord. You can write letters that encourage others to go forward in their faith. You can compassionately witness or sacrificially give to world missions. As you experience God's presence, living before Him in intimate fellowship, you can be assured that you have what it takes to be useful to God today. We can have this sense of purpose when we know eternal life is ours and that nothing can separate us from His everlasting love and life.[5]

You may wonder if you can really make a difference today. Have you experienced so many broken dreams or unfulfilled desires, coupled with sorrow and failure, that you doubt your ability to be usable? Remember that Elijah experienced debilitating disappointment and defeat that led him to the verge of suicide, yet he awoke on his last day to successfully make a profound difference in the lives of Elisha and the sons of the prophets. Consider that Jesus Christ is described as one "despised and rejected of men; a man of sorrows, and acquainted with grief" (Isaiah 53:3). Paul also knew rejection, sorrow, and criticism, yet he willingly risked spend-

> There is never an excuse for uselessness for Christ's cause.

ing himself for others and loving others more abundantly even though they loved him less (2 Corinthians 12:15). John Wesley was asked, "What would you do if you knew you were to die in three days?" Wesley wisely replied, "What I have already planned to do: preach here, meet with friends there, until the moment the Lord called me home." Wesley lived by the motto "Do all the good you can, by all the means you can, in all the places you can, at all the times you can, to all the people you can, in all the ways you can, for as long as you can!"

I received a letter from a ninety-two-year-old Christian woman who prays each day for our ministry in New York City. She had read a prayer letter in which I asked people to pray for our weekly Heritage of Faith radio program. In response, she sent a check for $780.00, the exact amount of one broadcast. There is never an excuse for uselessness for Christ's cause. One of Adoniram Judson's rules of life was "seek opportunities of making some sacrifice for the good of others." When the gift of God is yours, you have a divine reason for being right up to your last day.

THE COMFORT ZONE OF YOUTH

Elijah's confidence in heaven did not lead him to a presumptuous lifestyle but to a purpose-filled walk. One day is sufficient to accomplish something valuable. He saw no reason for discouragement even though he was living his last earthly day. In college a fellow student of mine named Christine contracted amyotrophic lateral sclerosis (ALS), commonly called Lou Gehrig's disease. Unable to walk, she wheeled onto the chapel platform to share her testimony—barring a miracle, she did not have long to live. Living on eternity's edge, Christine radiated incredible peace in the midst of human hopelessness. Her testimony of love for Christ stirred those of us living in the comfort zone of youth to devote ourselves to our Savior, Who conquered death. It may seem strange, but I left chapel that day almost wishing I could die too and be in the Savior's presence! Not long after, Christine did enter into the company of the One she longed to see, but her confidence in Christ's love and salvation during those final earthly days made an enduring imprint upon my heart.

Follow Your Dream with Assurance

Facing death's reality with assurance of eternal life will help us to overcome our fear and follow after our God-given dreams. We may fear stepping out of our comfort zone because of past failures. Maybe you have a history of pain and defeat that shouts for you to reject any risk. What terrifies you? Going to college? Getting married and starting a family? Pioneering a new business? Starting a church or going to the mission field? Writing a book?

Consider Rahab. Doing something seemingly simple, placing a scarlet cord in her window, was in fact the riskiest thing she had ever done. That decision would lead either to her salvation or to her death; but her living faith in the Lord led her to display that scarlet cord, and eventually both she and her family were saved from sure destruction. Even better, she became a legal descendant of Jesus Christ (Matthew 1:5)! Remember Esther. She faced her fears saying, "If I perish, I perish," because she knew that God had placed her in the king's court for "such a time" as that (Esther 4:16, 14). God used her to save her people from genocide and insure that the Messiah would be born. What would you attempt for God if you knew you would not fail? Is fear holding you back?

It is very difficult and risky for me to write this book. Who am I to write about how we should train leaders or disciple our generation? How much am I like Elijah, living each day as my last? Sometimes I feel more of a failure than a success in my attempts at such vital tasks. Many times I feel shallow in my personal walk with God. I am certainly not the model husband, parent, or pastor. But with God's help I am in the race, not quitting, putting my testimony on the line, and not giving in to fear. I am doing it because there is a burden upon my heart to live for Jesus Christ and "follow his steps" (1 Peter 2:21). Like Regina, I am going home, but I am not there yet, and as long as God gives me breath I long to "serve God acceptably with reverence and godly fear" (Hebrews 12:28). I can commit myself to the same loving heavenly Father that Jesus did when He completed with supreme assurance the most sacrificial act in all of history—dying upon the cross for the sins of the world. What are you waiting for? Do not fear stepping into the unknown. Stop hiding behind your doubts because you have no doubt that Jesus is yours and although much of life is an unknown, you know your eternal inheritance is forever secure: heaven is yours by the grace of Jesus Christ.

Death is not the end of life. Live today like Elijah—with confidence!—for Christ put death to death when He conquered the grave.

> Someday the silver cord will break,
> But oh, the joy when I shall wake
> Within the palace of the King!
> And I shall see him face to face,
> And tell the story—saved by grace![6]

Living with this assurance is basic to living on eternity's edge!

REFLECTIONS FOR TODAY

Make your calling and election sure. If you do not possess absolute confidence in Jesus Christ and His salvation, rest yourself now in His promise of eternal life. Read and reread Romans 10:9–13 and call upon the Lord to save you from eternal damnation. Get counsel from a pastor or Christian friend who has the settled assurance of eternal life.

MEMORIZE

1 John 5:12–13 "He that hath the Son hath life; and he that hath not the Son of God hath not life. These things have I written unto you that believe on the name of the Son of God; that ye may know that ye have eternal life, and that ye may believe on the name of the Son of God."

MEDITATE

Meditate on John 14:1–6. The entire section of John 14–17 is a discourse given by Jesus on the verge of His atoning death on the cross. Amazingly, one-third of John's Gospel (John 11–18) records Jesus' final day! Jesus gives us great comfort living His last hours upon earth.

1. In John 14:1, what is the key to having a heart that is not troubled?

2. What is Jesus' assurance in John 14:1–2?

3. In John 14:*2b*, what does Jesus tell the disciples He will do after leaving earth?

4. What is Jesus' answer to Thomas's question "How can we know the way?" (John 14:5–6)?

Sovereign Lord of life and death,
I praise You that my times are in Your hand and that
You give great assurance to those who come in faith to
You, that we will never perish, but one day be with You
in Your Father's house! Give me wisdom that I may
fulfill Your purpose today facing my every fear by the
power of the risen Christ. In Jesus' name, Amen.

9 Seeing Ultimate Reality . . . On Eternity's Edge

"If thou see me. . . . Elisha saw it" (2 Kings 2:10*b*, 12)

I n 1873 Hudson Taylor welcomed new missionaries to China and invited them to his hotel room. Without expectation, the novices cheerfully followed the veteran in his Chinese dress through the American, English, and French settlements of Shanghai. Taylor then led them into the heart of the Chinese city, where many missionaries feared to tread. "Heaps of malodorous refuse, fish, vegetables, muck from the streets, filth of all sorts . . . massive and unrelieved" bombarded the newcomers. Continuing to his room, they stumbled up an unlit, narrow staircase and finally entered the humble dwelling. "It consisted of a room about twelve feet square, innocent of any adornment." There they sat and Mr. Taylor read John 17, the Lord's high priestly prayer. He then asked what Jesus meant by His words spoken to His Father in prayer, "That the love wherewith thou hast loved me may be in them, and I in them" (John 17:26).[1]

As I ponder this scene, it seems clear that Taylor was testing the mettle of these new workers. Jesus described His Father's love in John 17:24, "Thou lovest me before the foundation of the world." Jesus then prayed for His followers to love Him with the same everlasting love that the Father has for His Son! This is impossible for any man to do and only God can answer that request! What the missionaries needed could not be seen, tasted, handled, or purchased. Who can muster an everlasting love for Jesus in our finite, deceitful hearts? This love abides naturally in no one; we can get it only from God Himself and by the power of Christ's life working in us. Without grasping this essential truth, those new servants would probably soon be back on a boat to their homeland.

THE POWER OF GOD: ONLY GOD CAN GIVE IT

In his final moments, Elijah issued Elisha his final exam to determine his grasp of ultimate reality. It comes in the form of a blank-check statement. "And it came to pass, when they were gone over, that Elijah said unto Elisha, Ask what I shall do for thee, before I be taken away from thee" (2 Kings 2:9). If you were to see a man open a river with the slap of a cloth who then asked, "What shall I do for you before I leave you, all you have to do is ask," what would you say? If I were in Elisha's shoes, I might have been tempted to respond in a shallow manner like, "I want three wishes." Thankfully, Elisha did not treat Elijah like a genie in a bottle.

Elisha made his desire known, "I pray thee, let a double portion of thy spirit be upon me" (2 Kings 2:9). He did not ask for earthly possessions or prestige. Having seen God's power manifested through Elijah's life, Elisha thirsted for this divine strength as well. The "double portion" speaks of receiving an inheritance, but not a material one.[2] Elisha was not requesting to be twice as great, or twice as strong, or twice as effective as Elijah.[3] Knowing Elijah had many disciples in the schools of the prophets, Elisha hungered to be acknowledged as his firstborn spiritual son. He wanted to continue Elijah's work of training the sons of the prophets and to turn the hearts of Israelites back to God with the same power that Elijah had. Elijah's inheritance was a God-ordained ministry represented by a mantle—humanly worthless but spiritually priceless. This was an invisible inheritance, and only God could give it to Elisha.

If Bethel were going to be restored to a place of God's real presence and if Jericho would again be a place where the power of God was revealed, if Elisha were going to overcome the spiritual battles of opposition from ungodly kings, prophets, and priests, and if he were to press on in reaching the hearts of those seven thousand souls who had not bowed to Baal, he needed to be filled with the Holy Spirit. This fullness is what we need too if we are going to see the invisible God work mightily through our lives.

PERSISTENT PRAYER FOR POWER

In a parable teaching the value of persistent prayer, Jesus told of a man in the middle of two friends, one rich and the other poor (Luke 11:5–13). The man in the middle unashamedly begged of his wealthy friend at midnight for three loaves of bread for his starving friend. Jesus taught that the rich man did not get up because of a strong friendship, "yet because of his importunity he will rise and give him as many as he needeth" (Luke 11:8). The point of this parable is that one with "importunity" will come to God with heartfelt urgency, will continue seeking God with shameless persistence, and will confess to God with sincere honesty his absolute need. The friend who needed bread did not quit begging from his affluent ally because he knew he had "nothing to set before" his companion in need (Luke 11:6). Therefore, he was shameless in his asking. We likewise

> **We have absolutely nothing to give anyone unless we are filled with the Holy Spirit of God.**

must come to God knowing that without Him we are nothing and have nothing. Jesus teaches us that the main point of our pleading with God is "how much more shall your heavenly Father give the Holy Spirit to them that ask him?" (Luke 11:13). We ought to pray regularly and even desperately for the power of the Holy Spirit.[4]

Many of God's people lack this importunity to ask God for His power. Laziness has set into our souls. "Ye have not, because ye ask not" (James 4:2). When we do ask, we are often driven by selfish motives to consume our requests on our own lust (James 4:2–3). Many who have been saved for many years are still weak and immature. Many believers content themselves with "low degrees of grace, and it is no easy matter to get them higher."[5]

In this same context of persistent prayer for the power of the Holy Spirit, Jesus taught, "Ask, and it shall be given you; seek, and ye shall find; knock, and it shall be opened unto you" (Luke 11:9). Jesus used the present tense in the words: *ask, seek,* and *knock,* implying continued action in each case. One who keeps asking receives. One who keeps seeking finds. One who keeps knocking has the door opened to him! One of the ways we are endued, filled, or controlled by the Holy Spirit is to ask God to fill us over and over again! May God give to us this kind of hungry heart. Only He can meet our deepest longings. We have absolutely nothing to give anyone unless we are filled with the Holy Spirit of God.

PURITY OF HEART

To properly answer Elijah's offer, "Ask what I shall do for thee," Elisha also needed a pure heart. Elijah's offer probed Elisha's inmost desires. What did this man really want? Underneath all your layers, what is it that you really hunger for? Undoubtedly, many legitimate material needs existed for Elijah and Elisha in their prophetic ministry.[6] Yet Elisha did not ask for "things" but for God Himself. "When all that heaven and earth could afford—all its riches, honors, pleasures—was spread like a scroll before him, and his choice from amongst all was freely offered, he asked for nothing but a double portion of the Holy Spirit . . . Elisha was prepared for the prophetic office."[7]

We also need purity of heart, and only God can give us the thorough cleansing we need. "Who shall ascend into the hill of the Lord? Or who shall stand in his holy place? He that hath clean hands, and a pure heart; who hath not lifted up his soul unto vanity, nor sworn deceitfully. . . . This is the generation of them that seek him, that seek thy face, O Jacob" (Psalm 24:3–4, 6). Anyone can be a part of this generation that seeks God. As believers, we must redirect our desires to what really counts. What do you want? We ought to say, "I want to walk in the Spirit with the affections of my heart directed to Jesus Christ, the Lover of my soul. I want to know that I am dead with Christ so that the life of Jesus will be manifested through my mortal flesh. I want to make the Word of God my meditation and delight so that I have wisdom to skillfully understand the knowledge of God. I want to be a doer of the Word and shine as a light for God. I want to be holy as God Himself is holy. I want to lead many lost souls to salvation in Jesus Christ." These are the desires of a pure heart that seeks after God. Elisha's desire for divine power and purity showed that he was ready to see what is truly important.

WHY MINISTRY IS HARD

As Elijah and Elisha continued on their way, Elijah told Elisha that if he saw him go into heaven, then he would attain his desire. Prayerfully read Elijah's final recorded earthly words: "And he said, Thou hast asked *a hard thing*: nevertheless, if thou see me when I am taken from thee, it shall be so unto thee; but if not, it shall not be so" (2 Kings 2:10; emphasis mine). Elisha asked a difficult thing, but it was the thing Elijah wanted him to ask. It was "hard" because it was something Elijah could not give. It was out of his control.[8] This is precisely why serving God is hard; what really needs to be done is outside our ability, and we don't like that! Those under our leadership, whether in our family, work, or church, have needs only God can supply. It humbles us that we cannot do what others ask, but it keeps us dependent on Him, pointing others to trust His infinite sufficiency. God's power is for God Himself to give. Only God can do it!

To attain his hard request, Elijah set a high standard beyond Elisha's natural ability, but not unattainable through God's infinite grace. He had to see Elijah depart. Not willing to leave his ministry in the hands of someone unworthy, the wise mentor challenged Elisha with what was supremely central for God-glorifying ministry: the capacity to see God at work in his world. Elisha needed a "spiritual vision and the manifestation from heaven could only be seen by eyes spiritually opened."[9] "To see the transactions of the spirit-world requires a spirit of no ordinary purity, and of no ordinary faith. No mere mortal eye could have beheld that fiery cortege."[10] Only God could do it and the lesson is clear: the amazing grace that begins the believer's life is required every day. "The outstanding lesson of this old time story is as plain as sunlight to us. It is that we cannot get on without God."[11] Daily and unquestionably, we need what only God can give.

DON'T BE DISTRACTED FROM HIM

Elisha could not be distracted with so much at stake. Likewise, to make our moments matter, we must "look not at the things which are seen, but at the things which are not seen: for the things which are seen are temporal; but the things which are not seen are eternal" (2 Corinthians 4:18). An eternal focus opens one's eyes to understand the true nature of life. This will sustain our desire to pursue an intimate relationship with God. Life's greatest realities cannot be perceived with physical eyes, for "our King eternal, immortal, invisible, the only wise God" is supreme truth (1 Timothy 1:17). Although we do not see Him, we love and believe Him as we look to Him with eyes of faith. We are commanded also to seek first the kingdom of God and His righteousness (Matthew 6:33). We do not grasp these privileges with our hands nor purchase them with money. Jesus desires the affection of our heart to be on Him, to worship and adore Him. Yet in the midst of family, work, and ministry we can be easily distracted. Daily we fight busyness that keeps us from Him. We allow newspapers and sports, television shows and DVD rentals, websites and e-mails to gobble time we could be spending in intimate fellowship with Christ.

Hurt Can Drive Us to God

I am sure that when King David fled from his son Absalom deep wounds preoccupied his soul. As his own son was toppling him from power, Shimei's curses rained down on David's head. Stones whizzed past his ears. Dust nearly blinded his eyes (2 Samuel 15–16). The hurt did not distract him from God but drove him to God in authentic worship. David actually wrote more than one psalm during that occasion.[12] And he saw the Lord, even through the cursing of Shimei and the rebellion of his son (2 Samuel 16:10). I like Psalm 3 because hostile circumstances swirled out of David's control, he saw the Lord as his personal friend, Who protected him and heard his voice in the midst of mounting trouble. David used eighteen personal pronouns in this brief eight-verse psalm, emphasizing that his heart was intertwined with God Himself. "But thou, O Lord, art a shield for me; my glory, and the lifter up of mine head" (Psalm 3:3). God's protection, abundance, and encouragement were real to David in spite of human defeat.

Determine to make time to read Scripture and to cry to God with your voice. Take out a pen like David did and write down the thoughts of your soul. Praise God. Thank Him, not necessarily for everything, but in whatever you are going through. Sing songs that move you near to God and help you sense His intimate presence. As with Elisha, what David needed could not be accessed by natural methods; he needed God's blessing to sustain him. David drew near to God in spite of deep inner grief in new surroundings. He lingered in God's presence in spite of an unknown future. And he challenged us all to see the Lord and lay hold of His salvation in Him even when He seems far from our range of vision. God, imperceptible to physical eyes, can be seen with a pure heart, and David knew he desperately needed Him.

Elisha Saw It

Think of this: Elisha actually saw chariots of fire and horses of fire from heaven escort Elijah from earth in an earthly body and into heaven by a whirlwind. Perhaps Elijah was in the middle of a sentence when suddenly he was swept away. The Scripture says, "And it came to pass, as they still went on, and talked, that, behold, there appeared a chariot of fire, and horses of fire, and parted them both asunder; and Elijah went up by a whirlwind into heaven. And Elisha saw it, and he cried. . . . And he saw him no more" (2 Kings 2:11–12). Elisha saw what Elijah required because God gave him the grace to see. He observed chariots and understood that a spiritual world war continually raged in the physical world around him.[13] He knew that the true strength and protection of a nation resides in Spirit-filled servants who make each day count for eternity. Elijah was the real chariot and horseman of Israel! Elisha got the necessary glimpse of Elijah's flight to God and understood that all people will live somewhere forever. Heaven is a real place! He also must have understood that those not believing in the living God will be eternally separated from Him. Elisha saw what Jacob saw in Bethel (Genesis 28:10–16). He saw what Elijah saw when God told him in a still small voice at Mount Horeb, "Return" (1 Kings 19:15). He saw what Hudson Taylor wanted those new missionaries to see in China. He saw that life's greatest reality is God Himself, at work in this world all around him. Although idolatry has claimed and

> **Life's greatest reality is God Himself.**

destroyed so many lives, God is still God, loving, strong, and fulfilling His purposes. With so much at stake, our labor will never be in vain in the Lord.

Our Age of Superficial Sight

What do you see? The tendency of our age is toward superficial sight. Images abound and we struggle with lusts for the images upon which our eyes can feast. Our passion must be to love and see the Lord. Our ability to experience God's love and distinguish spiritual reality is determined by our desire to have God's power and purity in our life. "Blessed are the pure in heart: for they shall see God" (Matthew 5:8). "Looking unto Jesus the author and finisher of our faith" (Hebrews 12:2). "Follow . . . holiness, without which no man shall see the Lord" (Hebrews 12:14). These verses all relate to our seeing "him who is invisible" today with eyes of faith (Hebrews 11:27). Our eyesight determines our worldview, our goals, our desires, and our spiritual condition. Our vision determines values and values shape our desires. And all of this influences our every decision. If all we see is the physical world around us, Jesus says our eye is evil (Matthew 6:22–23). If your life, your problems, your bills, your paycheck, your house, or your friends are your main point of reference, then you have an evil eye. Do you care about the world of anyone else? If you say, "I live for my paycheck. I can see that. I live for bread. I can eat that. I live to have security; I will enjoy that," then you have an evil eye ruled by the physical world. We need to love Jesus Christ with a love that only God can give to us. We need to see God at work as only God can help us to see. God is real, He is at work, and we need him. Seeing Him was ultimate reality to Elijah, Elisha, King David, and Hudson Taylor, and

He can be to us today as we live to love Him and see Him with eyes of faith, thirsting for God's power and purity on eternity's edge.

REFLECTIONS FOR TODAY

Seeing ultimate reality is fundamental to living on eternity's edge. Make God Himself your passion. In your devotions sing songs such as "A Passion for Thee" and "Nearer Still Nearer." Cleanse your hands, confess your sins, and claim God's forgiveness through the blood of Christ. Ask God to place in your heart a love for the Lord Jesus Christ equivalent to the everlasting love that the Father has for His Son.

MEMORIZE

John 17:24 "Father, I will that they also, whom thou hast given me, be with me where I am; that they may behold my glory, which thou hast given me: for thou lovest me before the foundation of the world."

MEDITATE

Meditate on John 17. As Jesus approached nearer to the cross, He came to His Father and offered His longest recorded prayer in Scripture. Reflect on the following verses.

1. In John 17:5 what did Jesus pray and whom did He see as the eternal center of the universe?

2. In verses 6–8, what had Jesus given to His disciples?

3. In verses 11–17, what did Jesus pray for His disciples?

4. In verses 24–26, what did Jesus pray for His disciples?

5. How can this apply to you as you consider the ultimate realities of life?

Dear eternal Lord,

I praise You that "blessed are the pure in heart: for they shall see God" (Matthew 5:8). Give me this heart that I might see You, even though You are invisible, and seeing You I would love You with all my heart and soul and strength. Teach me to love You, Lord Jesus, with the everlasting love of the Father working in me. Grant me Your grace that I might live for those eternal things that are not seen as I abide with You on eternity's edge. In Jesus' name, Amen.

10 Dropping the Mantle . . . On Eternity's Edge

"He took up also the mantle of Elijah. . . . The spirit of Elijah doth rest on Elisha" (2 Kings 2:13, 15)

When Elijah first met Elisha, he "cast his mantle upon him," for God had told Elijah that he must anoint Elisha to be a prophet in his place (1 Kings 19:16, 19). More than mere cloth, that mantle was the badge of Elijah's authority, and it represented the soul of his prophetic ministry. More valuable than earthly possessions or power, Elijah's mantle testified that the one possessing it lived on eternity's edge.

David Brainerd's diary reminds me of Elijah's mantle, and his memoirs have challenged many generations of God's servants. William Carey picked up the diary, which tells of incredible hardship during Brainerd's brief twenty-nine-year life, and went to India. Adoniram Judson read it and went to Burma. Henry Martyn read it and surrendered his heart for missionary service in India.

On his sickbed, Brainerd maximized his final moments by writing his unsaved brother. You can sense Brainerd's urgency that his sibling make his calling and election sure.

It is on the verge of eternity I now address you. . . . O, of what infinite importance is it that we be prepared for eternity! I have been just a-dying, now for more than a week . . . I have had clear views of eternity, have seen the blessedness of the godly, and have longed to share their happy state. . . . But O, what anguish is raised in my mind to think of an eternity for those who are Christless, for those who are mistaken and who bring their false hopes to the grave with them! The sight was so dreadful I could by no means bear it; my thoughts recoiled, and I said, under a more affecting sense than ever before, "Who can dwell with everlasting burnings?" . . . And for you, my dear brother, I have been particularly concerned; and have wondered I so much neglected conversing with you about your spiritual state at our last meeting. O, my brother, let me then beseech you now to examine whether you are indeed a new creature. . . . I declare, now I am dying, I would not have spent my life otherwise for the whole world. O, my dear brother, flee fleshly lusts, and the enchanting amusements, as well as the corrupt doctrines of the present day; and strive to please God[1].

ELIJAH'S ASCENT DANCES IN MY MIND

The scene of Elijah ascending in the chariot of fire by a whirlwind dances in my mind. I envision Elijah holding onto the chariot's side as he peers back at Elisha. When he hears Elisha cry, "My father, my father, the chariot of Israel, and the horsemen thereof," Elijah knows that Elisha "saw it" (2 Kings 2:12). Elijah's strong hand slowly lets go of the mantle; Elisha passed every test. The old prophet's last act was simply to release his authority to a deserving, God-called successor. Elisha meanwhile was overcome with anguish and tore his clothes. He loved Elijah as a father. He respected Elijah as a strong protector and defender for his nation. He then observed something fluttering down through the sky, but it was no meteor. Quietly, it landed upon the ground. He fixed his eyes and discovered the mantle the prophet used to throw about his shoulders. Prayerfully he picked it up and claimed it as his own.[2] Elisha, then standing on the wrong side of Jordan, called upon God and crossed miraculously through the Jordan River just as he had done with Elijah. Elisha's ministry as chief prophet began with a miracle identical to his mentor's—the opening of the Jordan River. This is proof that the power of God that rested upon Elijah was now upon Elisha. He then retraced the steps Elijah taught him to take, directly returning to Jericho (2 Kings 2:18–22) and then to Bethel (2 Kings 2:23–25), continuing where Elijah had left off. He would continue battling to bring God's law to needy hearts in those idolatrous centers and throughout the Northern Kingdom.

THE SPIRIT OF ELIJAH

Elisha did not request Elijah's mantle but that his spirit would be upon him. The mantle was the symbol; the spirit was the substance, the reality. Elijah was gone, but the spirit that consumed him lived on because the spirit of Elijah was in fact God's Spirit. The sons of the prophets recognized their new leader when they declared, "The spirit of Elijah doth rest on Elisha" (2 Kings 2:15). This does not mean that Elisha possessed Elijah's temperament, gifts, talents, or personality. Elijah did not attempt to make Elisha his clone. The spirit of Elijah that rested upon Elisha was a spirit of fervent prayer, walking in the presence of

> **It is your turn to take the mantle of service and transfer it to faithful men and women who will teach others also.**

God. It was a spirit of unqualified trust in God, even if it meant being fed by unclean ravens or starving widows (1 Kings 17:2–16). It was a spirit that never gave up on any individual, even if he were dead and lifeless (1 Kings 17:17–24). Elijah had a spirit of determination to loyally live for God, and Elisha now had it. He knew that the ministry of Elijah was not painless but that there was a great price to pay; service to God requires sacrifice. Many young people fizzle in ministry when hardship arises. The surrender of dedication—"Yes, Lord"—becomes "no" when difficulties escalate. The spirit of Elijah was a warrior spirit, leading others to remember God's power, following God, discipling the sons of the prophets, and training new leaders. Elisha was now the chariot of Israel, the real strength and protector of the land, and he could live with assurance knowing that God was at work all around him (2 Kings 13:14).[3]

Elisha owed a great debt to Elijah for the years of life poured into him. Likewise, we ought to be deeply grateful for those who have preceded us in gospel ministry. Thank God for the parent who prayed with you while you were young or for the unknown Sunday school teacher who labored for you during the week so that you would hear the message that Lord's day. Do not lose sight of faithful family members, pastors, evangelists, or seminary professors who emptied themselves in order to build you up in the faith. Now it is your turn to take the mantle of service and transfer it to faithful men and women who will teach others also.

I Am His Grandson

John Crabbe came to New York City to serve God. He was an experienced pastor and preacher and an incredible pianist. His wife had died and that was difficult for him, but God's joy was ever evident in his life. As I got to know him, I discovered that I was his spiritual "grandson." Pastor Crabbe had led a man to the Lord who pioneered the college campus ministry that the Lord used to reach me. Spiritually, I was part of Brother Crabbe's heritage and through the years he has lovingly called me "his grandson." He became an interim pastor of a Brooklyn church that refused to call him as a full-time pastor. They paid him barely anything for nearly two years. I watched to see what he would do. Would he complain for more money? Would he split the church and force them to vote on him to be a full-time pastor? He did neither. Rather than create any hurt or division in that church family, he kindly resigned and moved on to serve the Lord elsewhere. Since then, with fire under his feet and gospel passion in his heart, God has led him to assist missionaries, and he has made ninety trips to foreign countries! He is one of the most unpretentious men I have ever met as he humbly exudes God's love to commit himself to his Savior and Shepherd. He called me recently and said, "My son, I have been praying for you every day." He means it. This challenges me and encourages me to love God with all my heart. I am privileged to be his grandson in the faith, and I owe him more than I can ever repay.

It is difficult to drop the mantle for the next generation perhaps because it is so challenging to train someone else to pick it up. Elijah wisely accomplished both tasks. I have occasionally witnessed the older generation cling to their positions when the cause of God would be better served by the young. It is easy for an older pastor to resist stepping aside even when the church dwindles in strength or for a business owner to stay well past the time he ought to retire. Fear may motivate a person to stay longer in a ministry or job than he should. We need great wisdom to know the right time to lay the mantle down. It requires greater wisdom to train someone to continue what we have begun, but that is the way to live.

A NEW WELL-LIT DARK AGE

We are living in incredibly challenging times. Our society says it is ludicrous to see one worldview as being universally true for everyone. We are often told the Bible may contain bits of truth but that to say the Bible is true in every aspect and is the only truth for everyone, everywhere, is intellectual suicide. Our culture is becoming more and more hostile to a worldview that makes any claims of universal truth. Polytheism reigns supreme. Toleration and openness are near deities except when they are challenged by truth. "Tolerance now means that you're supposed to accept every belief as true."[4]

It is as if a new dark age has descended upon us: it is intellectual, it is modern, and it is very well illuminated. Just walk through Times Square at night: many diversions entertain the eyes, ears, and mind. Television screens send forth their glow at home all day and much of the night, computer screens at work and home often never go off, cell phones give continual access to images and to the Internet, and iPods allow people to listen to and watch what they want when they want it.[5] As knowledge increases, ignorance and even illiteracy to biblical truth increase even more.

The most important and influential culture-shaping institutions in our nation—the legal and educational systems, the medical and scientific communities, and the media and entertainment industries—no longer accept the validity of a biblical worldview. By worldview, I mean the answers to the basic questions of life relating to our

- Origin: where did I come from?

- Identity: who am I?

- Utility: what am I here to do?

- Morality: how then should I know and do right and not wrong?

- Destiny: where am I going?[6]

In the midst of our increasingly religiously pluralistic and secular society, Christianity will be forever relevant, for it is germane to these fundamental life questions. These questions are stubborn; they are basic to human nature. Every generation will ask them because no culture can change the fact that all men are image bearers of the one true God, and we have the right answers to these timeless queries. The recognition that Christianity is relevant—to the heart and the mind, in the home and in the marketplace—makes our job vital. As believers on the narrow road of Jesus Christ, we are often accused of being "narrow minded," but we are not! Christians ought to be the most open-minded and open-hearted of all people. Believing in Christ, the narrow way, should not translate into being intolerantly narrow minded. Yes, we are convinced that "there is none other name under heaven given among men, whereby we must be saved" (Acts 4:12), but we are open to learning what others believe so that we can compassionately reach them with the truth. More than ever we need to learn, live, love, and pass on the truth of God's Word to those coming behind us. This is what ultimately matters. Let us go forth in love, sharing these enduring answers found in the Word of God. Someday we will release our mantle and leave our legacy. Will we leave behind merely what someone can live on, or like Elijah, will we bequeath that which someone can live for? What exactly are you living for that you will leave behind?

Go for God

May God give us passionate enthusiasm and wisdom to understand life's brevity so that we live for what lasts eternally. There is one God, Who is the Creator of us all. One Savior died on the cross and shed His blood to forgive our sin and the sin of the world. One Man, the Lord Jesus Christ, bodily arose from the grave that we might be righteous and justified in the sight of our holy heavenly Father. We can and must serve God with the assurance of everlasting life like Elijah. Focus yourself like a laser to train and disciple your sons, daughters, new believers, and other faithful souls to be living sacrifices with passion for the will of God. Like Elijah, God wants us to experience Him daily, living loyally, remembering His power, and warring in the good fight of faith that lies before us. Grasping ultimate reality, we need to go for God, seeing Him Who is invisible and serving Him for the glory of our Lord Jesus Christ, for someday soon we must drop our mantle and leave eternity's edge for eternity itself.

Reflections for Today

Someday you will drop your mantle and leave eternity's edge for eternity itself. Make sure your life counts for eternity. Invest your time, talent, and treasure in what lasts: the Word of God, the souls of men, and God Himself.

Memorize

2 Peter 1:14 "Knowing that shortly I must put off this my tabernacle, even as our Lord Jesus Christ hath showed me."

Meditate

Meditate on 2 Peter 1:1–21. Second Peter is the apostle Peter's "mantle" that he writes before putting off his earthly body (see 2 Peter 1:13–14). Chapter 1 tells us about our faith.

The GIFT of faith, verses 1–4

1. How does one receive this precious gift of faith?

The GROWTH of faith, verses 5–11

2. Peter says we are to "add" to our life seven character qualities. What are they and why are they of such importance?

The GROUND of faith, verses 12–21

3. What is a more sure word than even the extraordinary experience Peter had in seeing the majesty of Jesus Christ and hearing God's voice from heaven? Why?

> *Dear Lord of life, love, and light,*
> *I praise You for the trustworthiness of Your eternal*
> *Word. Teach me daily to live for You, knowing that soon*
> *I will lay down this body of clay and dwell with You for*
> *all eternity. May my testimony encourage others to live*
> *on eternity's edge. Teach me to so live that I may receive*
> *the "crown of life" (James 1:12). Give me grace to finish*
> *my course and keep the faith to receive the "crown of*
> *righteousness" (2 Timothy 4:8). In Jesus' name, Amen.*

Notes

INTRODUCTION

1. D. A. Carson has an excellent discussion on "The Challenges of Contemporary Pluralism" in chapter 1 of *The Gagging of God* (Grand Rapids, Mich.: Zondervan, 1996), pp. 13–54. He states that the one absolute creed of philosophical pluralism is that "any notion that a particular ideological or religious claim is intrinsically superior to another is *necessarily* wrong."

2. Baal worship was not a new religion in Israel. It was the religion of the Canaanites before the conquest of Joshua. During the days of the judges, Baal worship still existed (Judges 6:30). During King David's reign, Baal worship was successfully eliminated, and to a large extent the nation of Israel experienced God's blessing because of this (Leon Wood, *Elijah, the Prophet of God,* [Des Plaines, Ill.: Regular Baptist Press, 1968] pp. 9–15).

3. The work by W. F. Albright, *Yahweh and the Gods of Canaan* (Winona Lake, Ind.: Eisenbrauns, 1994) is helpful in understanding the long struggle against this pagan fertility cult.

4. Frank Gaebelein, ed., *The Expositor's Bible Commentary*, vol. 6 (Grand Rapids, Mich.: Zondervan Publishing House, 1986), pp. 397, 399.

5. Robert Harris, Gleason Archer, and Bruce Waltke, eds. *Theological Wordbook of the Old Testament,* vol. 2 (Chicago: Moody Press, 1980), p. 793.

CHAPTER 1

1. John Thornbury, *Five Pioneer Missionaries: David Brainerd* (Carlisle, Pa.: The Banner of Truth Trust, 1993), p. 75.

2. A. W. Pink, *Elijah* (Carlisle, Pa.: The Banner of Truth, 1997), p. 21.

3. *Elohim* occurs over 2,500 times in the Old Testament and is translated "God." It is a plural name, hinting at the tri-unity of God. It means "the strong God of power." See Hebrews 11:3.

4. The name JEHOVAH occurs over 6,800 times in the Hebrew Scripture, is translated in all capitals in our King James Bible, and appears either as LORD or GOD. The name is derived from the verb "to be," emphasizing that God was, is, and ever will be. See Exodus 3:14.

5. James 5:17 gives us a glimpse into Elijah's life before we meet him in 1 Kings 17:1. James 5:17–18 says, "Elias was a man subject to like passions as we are, and he prayed earnestly that it might not rain: and it rained not on the earth by the space of three years and six months. And he prayed again, and the heaven gave rain, and the earth brought forth her fruit." Jesus Himself verifies this miracle by referring to it in His sermon in Nazareth (Luke 4:25).

6. God's law stated in plain language that He could turn the land of promise, of milk and honey, into a dust bowl of dryness if the people refused to hear and heed His Word. Elijah knew that Israel had reached this level of rejection of God's Word. Deuteronomy 11:16–17 says, "Take heed to yourselves, that your heart be not deceived, and ye turn aside, and serve other gods, and worship them; and then the Lord's wrath will be kindled against you, and he shut up the heaven, that there be no rain, and that the land yield not her fruit; and lest ye perish quickly from off the good land which the Lord giveth you." Deuteronomy 28:23–24 tells of the curse of severe famine that would come upon Israel if they did not obey God. "And thy heaven that is over thy head shall be brass, and the earth that is under thee shall be iron. The Lord shall make the rain of thy land powder and dust: from heaven shall it come down upon thee, until thou be destroyed." This shows undoubtedly that Elijah knew the written law of God given through Moses.

7. J. Allen Blair, *2 Peter: Devotional Studies on Living Faithfully* (Neptune, N.J.: Loizeaux Brothers, 1983), p. 19.

Chapter 2

1. Moody Adams, *The Titanic's Last Hero* (West Columbia, S.C.: The Olive Press, 1997), pp. 55, 69.

2. Adams, p. 15.

3. Adams, pp. 24, 25.

4. Two passages emphasize Jesus' nearness to us as He sits at the Father's right hand: "Seeing then that we have a great high priest, that is passed into the heavens, Jesus the Son of God, let us hold fast our profession. For we have not an high priest which cannot be touched with the feeling of our infirmities; but was in all points tempted like as we are, yet without sin. Let us therefore come boldly unto the throne of grace, that we may obtain mercy, and find grace to help in time of need" (Hebrews 4:14–16) and "But this man, because he continueth

ever, hath an unchangeable priesthood. Wherefore he is able also to save them to the uttermost that come unto God by him, seeing he ever liveth to make intercession for them. For such an high priest became us, who is holy, harmless, undefiled, separate from sinners, and made higher than the heavens" (Hebrews 7:24–26).

5. Theo Laetsch, *The Minor Prophets* (Saint Louis: Concordia Publishing House, 1956), pp. 98–99.

6. G. Campbell Morgan, *Hosea: The Heart and Holiness of God* (Grand Rapids, Mich.: Baker Book House, 1982), pp. 136, 138.

7. Laetsch, pp. 96–97.

8. David O. Beale, *In Pursuit of Purity* (Greenville, S.C.: Bob Jones University Press, 1986), pp. 14, 15.

9. Beale, pp. 154–55.

10. The Fundamentalist-Modernist controversy has been well documented: *Promise Unfulfilled*, Rolland McCune (Greenville, S.C.: Ambassador International, 2004), *The Tragedy of Compromise*, Earnest Pickering (Greenville, S.C.: Bob Jones University Press, 1994), as well as the previously cited *In Pursuit of Purity: American Fundamentalism Since 1850*, David O. Beale.

11. Sarah Tippitt, "U.S. Episcopal Church Approves First Openly Gay Bishop," *Washington Post*, August 5, 2003.

12. This passage reminds us that salvation is the work of God's grace alone and should motivate us to serve Him primarily to glorify Him and not for the outward results: "God hath not cast away his people which he foreknew. Wot ye not what the scripture saith of Elias? how he maketh intercession to God against Israel, saying, Lord, they have killed thy prophets, and digged down thine altars; and I am left alone, and they seek my life. But what saith the answer of God unto him? I have reserved to myself seven thousand men, who have not bowed the knee to the image of Baal. Even so then at this present time also there is a remnant according to the election of grace" (Romans 11:2–5).

CHAPTER 3

1. First Kings 16:29–17:1 tell how Ahab married Jezebel and then defied God by having "Hiel the Bethelite build Jericho: he laid the foundation thereof in Abiram his firstborn, and set up the gates thereof in his youngest son Segub, according to the word of the Lord which he spake by Joshua the son of Nun. And Elijah the Tishbite . . . said unto Ahab, As the Lord God of Israel liveth, before whom I stand, there shall not be dew nor rain these years, but according to my word." In order to prosper materially and appease Baal, Hiel sacrificed his two sons in the building project to that false deity.

2. Second Kings 1 centers on a story of Ahaziah, Ahab's successor, who was seeking the god Baal-zebub to heal him of his disease. Elijah rightly predicted his death while at the same time fearlessly calling down fire on 102 of the king's soldiers.

CHAPTER 4

1. The four river openings in Scripture are the Red Sea (Exodus 14:10–31), the Jordan River in the days of Joshua (Joshua 3:1–17), and these two in 2 Kings 2:1–15.

2. Joshua 5:13–15: "And it came to pass, when Joshua was by Jericho, that he lifted up his eyes and looked, and, behold, there stood a man over against him with his sword drawn in his hand: and Joshua went unto him, and said unto him, Art thou for us, or for our adversaries? And he said, Nay; but as captain of the host of the Lord am I now come. And Joshua fell on his face to the earth, and did worship, and said unto him, What saith my lord unto his servant? And the captain of the Lord's host said unto Joshua, Loose thy shoe from off thy foot; for the place whereon thou standest is holy. And Joshua did so."

3. Many verses teach us that life is war. Paul encourages us in 1 Timothy 1:18 to fight our spiritual battle with personal faith. Then he commands us to continually fight for the objective, historic faith found in Scripture in 1 Timothy 6:12.

4. John Piper, *Let the Nations Be Glad!* (Grand Rapids, Mich.: Baker Academic, 2003), p. 45.

5. Gary Smalley *If Only He Knew* (Grand Rapids, Mich.: Zondervan Publishing House, 1996), p. 80.

6. As I write this, our church is in a similar situation and I have claimed this verse again. This time, we have had to leave the Village Community School and are praying for an even bigger miracle and a more permanent solution to our space problems. The Lord has led us to institute "Project Rehoboth" to bring in sufficient funds to purchase our own place. We will be meeting temporarily in another school, but we pray God will give us a property for the church to own.

CHAPTER 5

1. Dr. and Mrs. Howard Taylor, *Hudson Taylor and the China Inland Mission: The Growth of a Soul* (Littleton, Colo.: Overseas Missionary Fellowship, 1998), pp. 70–71.

CHAPTER 6

1. Although this passage does not tell us that there were "sons of the prophets" in Gilgal, this city seems to have been Elijah's base of operation and sons of the prophets lived there, too. See 1 Samuel 7:16

and 2 Kings 4:38. The testimony of the Lord was established in Gilgal with twelve stones after Joshua crossed through the Jordan River (Joshua 4:19–24). Gilgal remained an encampment for the tabernacle, where sacrifices were offered through the time of Samuel and Saul (1 Samuel 10:5–8; 11:14–15).

2. Warren Wiersbe, *The Bible Exposition Commentary, Old Testament History* (Colorado Springs: Victor Books, 2003), p. 507.

3. Second Kings 6:1 says, "The sons of the prophets said unto Elisha, Behold now, the place where we dwell . . . is too strait for us." They began a successful building program to enlarge their training center (2 Kings 6:2–7).

4. W. E. Vine, *Vine's Complete Expository Dictionary* (Nashville: Thomas Nelson Publishers, 1996), p. 171.

5. Bill Hull, *The Disciple-Making Church* (Grand Rapids, Mich.: Fleming H. Revell, 1990), p. 18.

6. This is part of an e-mail I received from Florio Pierre on August 4, 2006.

7. John and Stasi Eldredge, *Captivating* (Nashville: Thomas Nelson, 2005), pp. 140–41.

8. Charles Spurgeon, Sermon entitled "A Pastoral Visit," No. 3103 on Philemon 1:2. Ages Librarian.

CHAPTER 7

1. Leon Wood, *Elijah, Prophet of God* (Des Plaines, Ill.: Regular Baptist Press, 1968), p. 151.

2. Isaac Watts, "Am I a Soldier of the Cross?" *Worship and Service Hymnal* (Carol Stream, Ill.: Hope Publishing Company, 1973).

3. F. B. Meyer, *Elijah and the Secret of His Power* (Fort Washington, Pa.: Christian Literature Crusade, 1978), p. 171.

4. C. S. Lewis, *The Screwtape Letters* (Uhrichsville, Ohio: Barbour and Company, Inc., 1995), pp. 76–77.

5. A. B. Bruce, *The Training of the Twelve* (Grand Rapids, Mich.: Kregel Publications, 1971), p. 29.

6. Bill Hull, *The Disciple-Making Church* (Grand Rapids, Mich.: Fleming H. Revell, 1990), p. 23.

7. C. F. Keil and F. Delitzsch, *Commentary on the Old Testament,* vol. 3 (Grand Rapids, Mich.: William B. Eerdmans), p. 294.

CHAPTER 8

1. Also read Job 38:1; Job 40:6; Ezekiel 1:4, which tell of God coming to Job and Ezekiel in a whirlwind to speak and personally reveal Himself to them.

2. Matthew Henry, *Matthew Henry's Commentary*, vol. 2 (McLean, Va.: MacDonald Publishing Company), p. 712.

3. Revelation 20:11–14 tells us of the great white throne judgment, which is reserved for unbelievers. The unsaved dead are resurrected in both body and soul to be judged and then cast into the lake of fire. See John Walvoord, *The Revelation of Jesus Christ: A Commentary by John F. Walvoord* (Chicago: Moody Press), pp. 305–10.

4. Second Kings 2:23 relates Elisha's experience in the city of Bethel soon after Elijah went up in the whirlwind. Young men mocked Elisha for believing that Elijah had indeed ascended in the chariot of fire. They also mocked Elisha's baldness, saying, "Go up, thou bald head, go up, thou bald head."

5. Two favorite passages that give the believer great assurance of salvation are John 10:27–29 and Romans 8:28–39.

6. Fanny Crosby, "Saved by Grace." *Living Hymns*, compiled and edited by Alfred B. Smith (Greenville, S.C.: Better Music Publications, 1988).

CHAPTER 9

1. Dr. and Mrs. Howard Taylor, *Hudson Taylor and the China Inland Mission: The Growth of a Work of God* (Littleton, Colo.: Overseas Missionary Fellowship, 1998), p. 246.

2. In Deuteronomy 21:15–17, Moses instructed a man with two wives to refuse favoring the son of the more beloved wife. When distributing his inheritance, he must not make the beloved wife's son the firstborn ahead of the hated. "He shall acknowledge the son of the hated for the firstborn, by giving him a *double portion* of all that he hath: for he is the beginning of his strength; the right of the firstborn is his."

3. George W. Truett, *The Prophet's Mantle* (Grand Rapids, Mich.: Baker Book House, 1948), p. 18.

4. We do not pray for the Holy Spirit's indwelling because He is a free gift given to us when we are saved. We are never told to pray for the indwelling of the Holy Spirit (1 Corinthians 6:19). We do need to beseech God for the Spirit's daily empowering.

5. Richard Baxter, *The Reformed Pastor* (Carlisle, Pa.: Banner of Truth Trust, 1997), p. 97.

6. One of the prophets would soon die and leave behind his wife with many debts (2 Kings 4:1). The sons of the prophets would need more

space at their school of the prophets and would not even have an ax with which to build. They borrowed tools, indicating they were not a wealthy group (2 Kings 6:1–7).

7. Alfred Edersheim, *Practical Truths from Elisha* (Grand Rapids, Mich.: Kregel Publications, 1982), p. 25.

8. Leon Wood, *Elijah, Prophet of God* (Des Plaines, Ill.: Regular Baptist Press, 1968), p. 154.

9. Edersheim, p. 27.

10. F. B. Meyer, *Elijah and the Secret of His Power* (Fort Washington, Pa.: Christian Literature Crusade, 1978), p. 172.

11. Truett, p. 23.

12. Besides Psalm 3, David also wrote Psalms 4 and 55 during his distress as he refreshed his heart by seeking God's heart.

13. This was not the only time Elisha saw horses and chariots of fire. When he and his servant were surrounded by the king of Syria's army, Elisha said to his terrified servant, "Fear not: for they that be with us are more than they that be with them. And Elisha prayed, and said, Lord, I pray thee, open his eyes, that he may see. And the Lord opened the eyes of the young man; and he saw: and, behold, the mountain was full of horses and chariots of fire round about Elisha" (2 Kings 6:16–17).

CHAPTER 10

1. John Thornbury, *Five Pioneer Missionaries* (Carlisle, Pa.: The Banner of Truth Trust, 1993), pp. 74, 75.

2. C. H. Spurgeon, Sermon entitled "Preparing to Depart" (Ages Digital Library, 1999), p. 686.

3. Second Kings 13:14 tells us that King Joash's words to Elisha at his death were the exact words that Elisha spoke at Elijah's departure: "Now Elisha was fallen sick of his sickness whereof he died. And Joash the king of Israel came down unto him, and wept over his face, and said, O my father, my father, the chariot of Israel, and the horsemen thereof."

4. Norman Geisler and Frank Turek, *I Don't Have Enough Faith to Be an Atheist* (Wheaton, Ill.: Crossway Books, 2004), p. 46.

5. John G. Stackhouse Jr., "The Christian Church in the New Dark Age: Illiteracy, Aliteracy, and the Word of God," *Evangelical Landscapes: Facing Critical Issues of the Day* (Grand Rapids, Mich.: Baker, 2002), pp. 89–102.

6. Geisler and Turek, p. 20.